Studies in World History Vol. 1

DR. JAMES STOBAUGH

Creation Through
the Age of Discovery
{4004 BC to AD 1500}

GEOGRAPHY   ECONOMICS   GOVERNMENT   HISTORY   RELIGION

MENT   HISTORY   GEOGRAPHY   RELIGION   ECONOMICS   HISTORY

TEACHER GUIDE

 Includes: Answer Keys

 Daily Calendar

 Daily Discussion Questions

 Weekly Exams

First printing: March 2014

Copyright © 2014 by Master Books®. All rights reserved. No part of this book may be used or reproduced in any manner whatsoever without written permission of the publisher, except in the case of brief quotations in articles and reviews. For information write:

Master Books®, P.O. Box 726, Green Forest, AR 72638

Master Books® is a division of the New Leaf Publishing Group, Inc.

ISBN: 978-0-89051-791-8

Unless otherwise noted, Scripture quotations are from the New King James Version of the Bible.

Printed in the United States of America

Please visit our website for other great titles:
www.masterbooks.net

For information regarding author interviews,
please contact the publicity department at (870) 438-5288

Master
Books®
A Division of New Leaf Publishing Group
www.masterbooks.net

Where Creation Inspires Education

Since 1975, Master Books has been providing educational resources based on a biblical worldview to students of all ages. At the heart of these resources is our firm belief in a literal six-day creation, a young earth, the global Flood as revealed in Genesis 1–11, and other vital evidence to help build a critical foundation of scriptural authority for everyone. By equipping students with biblical truths and their key connection to the world of science and history, it is our hope they will be able to defend their faith in a skeptical, fallen world.

If the foundations are destroyed, what can the righteous do?
Psalm 11:3; NKJV

As the largest publisher of creation science materials in the world, Master Books is honored to partner with our authors and educators, including:

Ken Ham of Answers in Genesis

Dr. John Morris and Dr. Jason Lisle of the Institute for Creation Research

Dr. Donald DeYoung and Michael Oard of the Creation Research Society

Dr. James Stobaugh, John Hudson Tiner, Rick and Marilyn Boyer, Dr. Tom Derosa, and so many more!

Whether a pre-school learner or a scholar seeking an advanced degree, we offer a wonderful selection of award-winning resources for all ages and educational levels.

But sanctify the Lord God in your hearts, and always be ready
to give a defense to everyone who asks you a reason for the hope
that is in you, with meekness and fear.
1 Peter 3:15; NKJV

Permission to Copy

Lessons for a 34-week course!

Overview: This *Studies in World History Volume 1 Teacher Guide* contains materials for use with *Studies in World History Volume 1*. Materials are organized by chapter in the following sections:

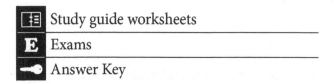

📋	Study guide worksheets
E	Exams
🗝	Answer Key

Features: Each suggested weekly schedule has five easy-to-manage lessons that combine reading, worksheets, and optional exams. Worksheets and exams are perforated and three-hole punched – materials are easy to tear out, hand out, grade, and store. You are encouraged to adjust the schedule and materials needed to best work within your educational program.

Workflow: Students will read the pages in their book and then complete each section of the PLP. Exams are given at regular intervals with space to record each grade. If used with younger students, they may be given the option of taking open-book exams.

Lesson Scheduling: Space is given for assignment dates. There is flexibility in scheduling. For example, the parent may opt for a M, W, F schedule, rather than a M–F schedule. Each week listed has five days but due to vacations the school work week may not be M–F. Adapt the days to your school schedule. As the student completes each assignment, he/she should put an "X" in the box.

🕐	Approximately 20 to 30 minutes per lesson, five days a week
🗝	Includes answer keys for worksheets and exams
📋	Worksheets for each section
↻	Exams are included to help reinforce learning and provide assessment opportunities
📄	Designed for grades 7 to 9 in a one-year course to earn 1 Social Studies credit

Dr. James Stobaugh was a Merrill Fellow at Harvard and holds degrees from Vanderbilt and Rutgers universities, and Princeton and Gordon-Conwell seminaries. An experienced teacher, he is a recognized leader in homeschooling and has published numerous books for students and teachers, including a high school history series (American, British, and World), as well as a companion high school literature series. He and his wife Karen have homeschooled their four children since 1985.

Contents

Introduction

The junior high student will see history come to life no matter what his or her pace or ability. Developed by Dr. James Stobaugh, these courses grow in difficulty with each year, preparing students for high school work. This is a comprehensive examination of history, geography, economics, and government systems. This educational set equips students to learn from a starting point of God's creation of the world and move forward with a solid biblically-based worldview. Volume 1 covers the Fertile Crescent, Egypt, India, China, Japan, Greece, Christian history, and more.

How this course has been developed:

1. Chapters: This course has 34 chapters (representing 34 weeks of study).

2. Lessons: Each chapter has five lessons, taking approximately 20 to 30 minutes each. There is a short reading followed by discussion questions. Some questions require a specific answer from the text, while others are more open-ended, leading students to think "outside the box."

3. Weekly exams: This Teacher Guide includes two optional exams for each chapter.

4. Student responsibility: Responsibility to complete this course is on the student. Students are to complete the readings every day, handing their responses in to a parent or teacher for evaluation. This course was designed for students to practice independent learning.

5. Grading: Students turn in assignments to a parent or teacher for grading.

Throughout the student text are the following components:

1. First thoughts: Background on the historical period.

2. Discussion questions: Questions based generally on Bloom's Taxonomy.

3. Concepts: Terms, concepts, and theories to be learned that are bolded for emphasis. Most are listed on the first page of the chapter and in the glossary.

4. History makers: A person(s) who clearly changed the course of history.

5. Historical debate: An examination of historical theories surrounding a period or topic.

First Semester Suggested Daily Schedule

Date	Day	Assignment	Due Date	✓	Grade
		First Semester-First Quarter			

Chapter 1: The Fertile Cresent: Nomads to Farmers

Mesopotamia, a civilization whose geography made all the difference in the world, was thriving before all other civilizations, but remained in the crosshairs of future civilizations, some coming, others going, but all in the mood to conquer this beautiful land along the way, whom many think was the Garden of Eden.

Date	Day	Assignment	Due Date	✓	Grade
Week 1	Day 1	Read **Lesson 1 — History: The Fertile Crescent** • Student Book (SB) • Answer Discussion Question Page 21 • Lesson Planner (LP)			
	Day 2	Read **Lesson 2 — Geography: A River Civilization** (SB) Answer Discussion Question Page 22 (LP)			
	Day 3	Read **Lesson 3 — Government: Rule of Law** (SB) Answer Discussion Question Page 23 (LP)			
	Day 4	Read **Lesson 4 — Economy: The Development ... of Time** (SB) Answer Discussion Question Page 24 (LP)			
	Day 5	Read **Lesson 5 — Religion: Polytheism** (SB) Answer Discussion Question Page 25 (LP) Optional **Chapter 1 Exam** 1 or 2 Page 227-228 (LP)			

Chapter 2: A River Runs North: Nile

As vulnerable as the geography made the Mesopotamian civilizations, geography in Egypt made the Nile region more or less isolated, which will have a significant impact on this most extraordinary civilization that grew in the delta on the north part of the Nile.

Date	Day	Assignment	Due Date	✓	Grade
Week 2	Day 6	Read **Lesson 1 — History: The Fertile River Valley** (SB) Answer Discussion Question Page 27 • (LP)			
	Day 7	Read **Lesson 2 — Geography: Between Red and Black Land** (SB) Answer Discussion Question Page 28 (LP)			
	Day 8	Read **Lesson 3 — Government: Pharoah** (SB) Answer Discussion Question Page 29 (LP)			
	Day 9	Read **Lesson 4 — Ramses II and the Exodus** (SB) Answer Discussion Question Page 30 (LP)			
	Day 10	Read **Lesson 5 — Egyptian Culture** (SB) Answer Discussion Question Page 31 (LP) Optional **Chapter 2 Exam** 1 or 2 Page 229-230 (LP)			

Chapter 3: God's Precious Treasure: Prospering in a Hostile Place

Israel, the Promised Land, initially promised milk and honey, hope and covenant, to a people desperately in need of both. But, in the years ahead, this people would have to fight time and time again, to keep what God so graciously gifted them.

Date	Day	Assignment	Due Date	✓	Grade
Week 3	Day 11	Read **Lesson 1 — Overview** (SB) Answer Discussion Question Page 33 • (LP)			
	Day 12	Read **Lesson 2 — Abraham: Nomadic Food, ...** (SB) Answer Discussion Question Page 34 (LP)			
	Day 13	Read **Lesson 3 — Israel: Geography** (SB) Answer Discussion Question Page 35 (LP)			
	Day 14	Read **Lesson 4 — Israel: Government** (SB) Answer Discussion Question Page 36 (LP)			
	Day 15	Read **Lesson 5 — Israel: Religion** (SB) Answer Discussion Question Page 37 (LP) Optional **Chapter 3 Exam** 1 or 2 Page 231-232 (LP)			

Date	Day	Assignment	Due Date	✓	Grade

Chapter 4: Indus Valley: Religion and Culture Are United

The religion, not geography, of South Asia was, and will remain, the primary culture-creating factor in all aspects of society.

Date	Day	Assignment	Due Date	✓	Grade
Week 4	Day 16	Read **Lesson 1 — Indus Valley Civilization** (SB) Answer Discussion Question Page 39 • (LP)			
	Day 17	Read **Lesson 2 — Aryan Civilization Daily Life** (SB) Answer Discussion Question Page 40 (LP)			
	Day 18	Read **Lesson 3 — Age of Empires** (SB) Answer Discussion Question Page 41 (LP)			
	Day 19	Read **Lesson 4 — Historical Essay** (SB) Answer Discussion Question Page 42 (LP)			
	Day 20	Read **Lesson 5 — The Panchatantra** (SB) Answer Discussion Question Page 43 (LP) Optional **Chapter 4 Exam** 1 or 2 Page 233-234 (LP)			

Chapter 5: Ancient China: Technology Triumphs

China is and will remain a civilization of contrasts: It based its economy on innovative technology but was always ambivalent about connecting with outsiders; it explored exotic lands but was not keen on trading with the lands; it was rich in religious tradition but eventually embraced a sort of atheism.

Date	Day	Assignment	Due Date	✓	Grade
Week 5	Day 21	Read **Lesson 1 — Chinese Geography** (SB) Answer Discussion Question Page 45 • (LP)			
	Day 22	Read **Lesson 2 — Traditional Chinese Life** (SB) Answer Discussion Question Page 46 (LP)			
	Day 23	Read **Lesson 3 — Chinese Weapons** (SB) Answer Discussion Question Page 47 (LP)			
	Day 24	Read **Lesson 4 — Chinese Age of Exploration** (SB) Answer Discussion Question Page 48 (LP)			
	Day 25	Read **Lesson 5 — Women in Ancient China** (SB) Answer Discussion Question Page 49 (LP) Optional **Chapter 5 Exam** 1 or 2 Page 235-236 (LP)			

Chapter 6: Mongol Hordes: Nomads by Choice

The Mongols, one of the first people groups to prefer a nomadic existence, to an agrarian one, effectively conquered most of the known world but had no notion of how to rule it.

Date	Day	Assignment	Due Date	✓	Grade
Week 6	Day 26	Read **Lesson 1 — Overview** (SB) Answer Discussion Question Page 51 • (LP)			
	Day 27	Read **Lesson 2 — Kublai Khan** (SB) Answer Discussion Question Page 52 (LP)			
	Day 28	Read **Lesson 3 — Mongol Army** (SB) Answer Discussion Question Page 53 (LP)			
	Day 29	Read **Lesson 4 — Life in the Steppes** (SB) Answer Discussion Question Page 54 (LP)			
	Day 30	Read **Lesson 5 — The Rise of Confederations** (SB) Answer Discussion Question Page 55 (LP) Optional **Chapter 6 Exam** 1 or 2 Page 237-238 (LP)			

Chapter 7: Early Japan: Identity Crisis

Japan was the only ancient civilization that was able to isolate itself from the outside. It experienced consistent growth and prosperity for two centuries, but was ill-prepared for the radical social changes that the end of this isolation would bring to it in its kaleidoscopic future.

Date	Day	Assignment	Due Date	✓	Grade
Week 7	Day 31	Read **Lesson 1 — Overview** (SB) Answer Discussion Question Page 57 • (LP)			
	Day 32	Read **Lesson 2 — Government** (SB) Answer Discussion Question Page 58 (LP)			
	Day 33	Read **Lesson 3 — Japanese Economy** (SB) Answer Discussion Question Page 59 (LP)			
	Day 34	Read **Lesson 4 — Social Structure** (SB) Answer Discussion Question Page 60 (LP)			
	Day 35	Read **Lesson 5 — Sakoku: Isolationism as a Political Policy** (SB) Answer Discussion Question Page 61 (LP) Optional **Chapter 7 Exam** 1 or 2 Page 239-240 (LP)			

Chapter 8: Ancient Religion: To Tame the Savageness of Man

Christianity is not the oldest, but it is the most popular religion in history. But in a world of so many divergent faiths, it will be vital that future Christian believers understand the roots of its competitors for the hearts and souls of mankind.

Date	Day	Assignment	Due Date	✓	Grade
Week 8	Day 36	Read **Lesson 1 — Zoroastrianism** (SB) Answer Discussion Question Page 63 • (LP)			
	Day 37	Read **Lesson 2 — Confucianism** (SB) Answer Discussion Question Page 64 (LP)			
	Day 38	Read **Lesson 3 — Buddhism** (SB) Answer Discussion Question Page 65 (LP)			
	Day 39	Read **Lesson 4 — Taoism** (SB) Answer Discussion Question Page 66 (LP)			
	Day 40	Read **Lesson 5 — Hinduism** (SB) Answer Discussion Question Page 67 (LP) Optional **Chapter 8 Exam** 1 or 2 Page 241-242 (LP)			

Chapter 9: Greece: Made Gentle the Life of Man

The Athenian Greeks grasped the notion that democracy was the best government, but unfortunately they could not sustain that world view beyond one city state. In one long era — but what an era it was — perhaps no ancient people had more effect on the future of the world than that little city-state, on the edge of the world!

Date	Day	Assignment	Due Date	✓	Grade
Week 9	Day 41	Read **Lesson 1 — History** (SB) Answer Discussion Question Page 69 • (LP)			
	Day 42	Read **Lesson 2 — Geography** (SB) Answer Discussion Question Page 70 (LP)			
	Day 43	Read **Lesson 3 — The Trojan Wars** (SB) Answer Discussion Question Page 71 (LP)			
	Day 44	Read **Lesson 4 — Battle of Thermopylae: 300 Spartans** (SB) Answer Discussion Question Page 72 (LP)			
	Day 45	Read **Lesson 5 — Golden Age of Pericles** (SB) Answer Discussion Question Page 73 (LP) Optional **Chapter 9 Exam** 1 or 2 Page 243-244 (LP)			

Date	Day	Assignment	Due Date	✓	Grade
		First Semester-Second Quarter			

Chapter 10: Greek Drama: Art Is Life
The Greeks grasp the essence of life like no one else and place that in the lap of eternity.

Date	Day	Assignment	Due Date	✓	Grade
Week 1	Day 46	Read **Lesson 1 — Greek Art** (SB) Answer Discussion Question Page 75 • (LP)			
	Day 47	Read **Lesson 2 — Greek Drama** (SB) Answer Discussion Question Page 76 (LP)			
	Day 48	Read **Lesson 3 — Greek Drama** (SB) Answer Discussion Question Page 77 (LP)			
	Day 49	Read **Lesson 4 — Euripides: Greek Poet** (SB) Answer Discussion Question Page 78 (LP)			
	Day 50	Read **Lesson 5 — Greek Sculpture** (SB) Answer Discussion Question Page 79 (LP) Optional **Chapter 10 Exam** 1 or 2 Page 245-246 (LP)			

Chapter 11: Alexander the Great: Descended from Hercules
No man has so indelibly marked an area of the world with his life in such a short time as Alexander did — his conquests still appear in nation marks, cultural evidences, and religious preferences.

Date	Day	Assignment	Due Date	✓	Grade
Week 2	Day 51	Read **Lesson 1 — Alexander the Great** (SB) Answer Discussion Question Page 81 • (LP)			
	Day 52	Read **Lesson 2 — Military Campaigns** (SB) Answer Discussion Question Page 82 (LP)			
	Day 53	Read **Lesson 3 — Alexander's Legacy** (SB) Answer Discussion Question Page 83 (LP)			
	Day 54	Read **Lesson 4 — How "Great?" Was Alexander?** (SB) Answer Discussion Question Page 84 (LP)			
	Day 55	Read **Lesson 5 — Alexandria** (SB) Answer Discussion Question Page 85 (LP) Optional **Chapter 11 Exam** 1 or 2 Page 247-248 (LP)			

Chapter 12: Roman Empire: The Bridge To Modern Times
The Roman Empire was the largest empire, to date, in world history, and it was to last a thousand years; however, its greatest claim to fame were its roads, aqueducts, and buildings that have lasted three thousand years.

Date	Day	Assignment	Due Date	✓	Grade
Week 3	Day 56	Read **Lesson 1 — History: the Beginning** (SB) Answer Discussion Question Page 87 • (LP)			
	Day 57	Read **Lesson 2 — Government** (SB) Answer Discussion Question Page 88 (LP)			
	Day 58	Read **Lesson 3 — Religion: A Little of This, a Little of That** (SB) Answer Discussion Question Page 89 (LP)			
	Day 59	Read **Lesson 4 — Sociology: Roman Family** (SB) Answer Discussion Question Page 90 (LP)			
	Day 60	Read **Lesson 5 — Economics: Agrarian Base** (SB) Answer Discussion Question Page 91 (LP) Optional **Chapter 12 Exam** 1 or 2 Page 249-250 (LP)			

Chapter 13: Christianity: The People of the Way

The first and second century Church created patterns that are still functioning today. Struggling in a hostile place, the Church still managed, against overwhelming odds, to conquer the intellectual and religious world of its time!

Date	Day	Assignment	Due Date	✓	Grade
Week 4	Day 61	Read **Lesson 1 — Christianity: Overview** (SB) Answer Discussion Question Page 93 • (LP)			
	Day 62	Read **Lesson 2 — Christianity: Demographics** (SB) Answer Discussion Question Page 94 (LP)			
	Day 63	Read **Lesson 3 — Early Church Services** (SB) Answer Discussion Question Page 95 (LP)			
	Day 64	Read **Lesson 4 — Primary Source Material** (SB) Answer Discussion Question Page 96 (LP)			
	Day 65	Read **Lesson 5 — Sociology: Persecution** (SB) Answer Discussion Question Page 97 (LP) Optional **Chapter 13 Exam** 1 or 2 Page 251-252 (LP)			

Chapter 14: Christianity: The World Turned Upside-Down

Never had a world known a faith or a people who made the blind walk, the deaf hear, who equally valued man and woman alike, who were willing to die for that faith, and who loved an Empire into the everlasting Kingdom.

Date	Day	Assignment	Due Date	✓	Grade
Week 5	Day 66	Read **Lesson 1 — Women in the Early Church** (SB) Answer Discussion Question Page 99 • (LP)			
	Day 67	Read **Lesson 2 — Evangelism in the Early Church** (SB) Answer Discussion Question Page 100 (LP)			
	Day 68	Read **Lesson 3 — Heresy in the Early Church** (SB) Answer Discussion Question Page 101 (LP)			
	Day 69	Read **Lesson 4 — The Canon** (SB) Answer Discussion Question Page 102 (LP)			
	Day 70	Read **Lesson 5 — Desert Fathers: Christian Radicals** (SB) Answer Discussion Question Page 103 (LP) Optional **Chapter 14 Exam** 1 or 2 Page 253-254 (LP)			

Chapter 15: Age of Augustine: The Church Prospers in a Hostile Culture

The barbarians ravaged, conquered, and humiliated the Romans, but the Roman Christians conquered the barbarians with their love.

Date	Day	Assignment	Due Date	✓	Grade
Week 6	Day 71	Read **Lesson 1 — Young Augustine** (SB) Answer Discussion Question Page 105 • (LP)			
	Day 72	Read **Lesson 2 — Augustine's Conversion** (SB) Answer Discussion Question Page 106 (LP)			
	Day 73	Read **Lesson 3 — Pastor Augustine** (SB) Answer Discussion Question Page 107 (LP)			
	Day 74	Read **Lesson 4 — New Heresies** (SB) Answer Discussion Question Page 108 (LP)			
	Day 75	Read **Lesson 5 — Waiting for the Barbarian** (SB) Answer Discussion Question Page 109 (LP) Optional **Chapter 15 Exam** 1 or 2 Page 255-256 (LP)			

Chapter 16: African Kingdoms: Benign Neglect

The Sub-Saharan Africans were enjoying exotic spices from the East Indies two hundred years before Marco Polo was born; their cities rivaled Paris and Berlin five hundred years before these cities were founded; their commercial acumen surpassed even the most astute medieval burger.

Date	Day	Assignment	Due Date	✓	Grade
	Day 76	Read **Lesson 1 — Overview** (SB) Answer Discussion Question Page 111 • (LP)			
	Day 77	Read **Lesson 2 — Ghana** (SB) Answer Discussion Question Page 112 (LP)			
Week 7	Day 78	Read **Lesson 3 — Economics: Controlling the Gold Trade** (SB) Answer Discussion Question Page 113 (LP)			
	Day 79	Read **Lesson 4 — Mali** (SB) Answer Discussion Question Page 114 (LP)			
	Day 80	Read **Lesson 5 — History of Timbuktu** (SB) Answer Discussion Question Page 115 (LP) Optional **Chapter 16 Exam** 1 or 2 Page 257-258 (LP)			

Chapter 17: Ancient North America: Hunter Gatherers

The North American mound builders were sipping coffee and smoking tobacco while Europeans were sleeping in mud huts on the Danube River; splendid isolation would create an unparalleled empire of native people.

Date	Day	Assignment	Due Date	✓	Grade
	Day 81	Read **Lesson 1 — The First Americans** (SB) Answer Discussion Question Page 117 • (LP)			
	Day 82	Read **Lesson 2 — Ancient Burial Mounds** (SB) Answer Discussion Question Page 118 (LP)			
Week 8	Day 83	Read **Lesson 3 — Native American Culture** (SB) Answer Discussion Question Page 119 (LP)			
	Day 84	Read **Lesson 4 — Sociology: Kinship** (SB) Answer Discussion Question Page 120 (LP)			
	Day 85	Read **Lesson 5 — Anthropology: The Impact of the Horse** (SB) Answer Discussion Question Page 121 (LP) Optional **Chapter 17 Exam** 1 or 2 Page 259-260 (LP)			

Chapter 18: Ancient South and Central America: The End of All Things

Today the Mayan civilization dominates the Yucatan Peninsula as completely as it did fifteen hundred years ago; curious overweight North American visitors walk on the paths that once led nervous victims to their untimely deaths above sacrificial altars.

Date	Day	Assignment	Due Date	✓	Grade
	Day 86	Read **Lesson 1 — Geography of South America** (SB) Answer Discussion Question Page 123 • (LP)			
	Day 87	Read **Lesson 2 — Centers of Civilizations in the Americas** (SB) Answer Discussion Question Page 124 (LP)			
Week 9	Day 88	Read **Lesson 3 — Overview of People Groups** (SB) Answer Discussion Question Page 125 (LP)			
	Day 89	Read **Lesson 4 — What Happened to the Maya?** (SB) Answer Discussion Question Page 126 (LP)			
	Day 90	Read **Lesson 5 — The Incas: A Mountain People** (SB) Answer Discussion Question Page 127 (LP) Optional **Chapter 18 Exam** 1 or 2 Page 261-262 (LP)			
		Mid-Term Grade			

Second Semester Suggested Daily Schedule

Date	Day	Assignment	Due Date	✓	Grade
		Second Semester-Third Quarter			

Chapter 19: Byzantium: Saints Standing in God's Holy Light
For a thousand years, a sophisticated people guarded the Bosporus Strait and unknowingly only allowed the most deadly of invaders to pass: the Bubonic Plague.

Date	Day	Assignment	Due Date	✓	Grade
Week 1	Day 91	Read **Lesson 1 — Byzantium** (SB) Answer Discussion Question Page 129 • (LP)			
	Day 92	Read **Lesson 2 — The Emperor Justinian** (SB) Answer Discussion Question Page 130 (LP)			
	Day 93	Read **Lesson 3 — Geography: Bosporus Strait** (SB) Answer Discussion Question Page 131 (LP)			
	Day 94	Read **Lesson 4 — Eastern Orthodox Church** (SB) Answer Discussion Question Page 132 (LP)			
	Day 95	Read **Lesson 5 — The Black Death** (SB) Answer Discussion Question Page 133 (LP) Optional **Chapter 19 Exam** 1 or 2 Page 263-264 (LP)			

Chapter 20: Early Russia: A People Formed by Geography
Russia turned its eyes to the West in this era and has never looked again, seriously, to the East.

Date	Day	Assignment	Due Date	✓	Grade
Week 2	Day 96	Read **Lesson 1 — History: Kievan Russians** (SB) Answer Discussion Question Page 135 • (LP)			
	Day 97	Read **Lesson 2 — Tatars** (SB) Answer Discussion Question Page 136 (LP)			
	Day 98	Read **Lesson 3 — Geography: Vastness** (SB) Answer Discussion Question Page 137 (LP)			
	Day 99	Read **Lesson 4 — Primary Source: The Novgorod First Chronicle** (SB) Answer Discussion Question Page 138 (LP)			
	Day 100	Read **Lesson 5 — Demographics: Moscow** (SB) Answer Discussion Question Page 139 (LP) Optional **Chapter 20 Exam** 1 or 2 Page 265-266 (LP)			

Chapter 21: Eastern Europeans: A People Conflicted
Eastern Europe gains its identity crisis that it retains even today: Is it Christian? Islamic? Nomadic? Agricultural? Hungarian? Austrian? Slavic? A world war would be fought to resolve that issue, but the region is as conflicted today as it was 500 years ago.

Date	Day	Assignment	Due Date	✓	Grade
Week 3	Day 101	Read **Lesson 1 — Overview** (SB) Answer Discussion Question Page 141 • (LP)			
	Day 102	Read **Lesson 2 — Primary Source** (SB) Answer Discussion Question Page 142 (LP)			
	Day 103	Read **Lesson 3 — The Huns** (SB) Answer Discussion Question Page 143 (LP)			
	Day 104	Read **Lesson 4 — Attila** (SB) Answer Discussion Question Page 144 (LP)			
	Day 105	Read **Lesson 5 — Hungarian Cossacks** (SB) Answer Discussion Question Page 145 (LP) Optional **Chapter 21 Exam** 1 or 2 Page 267-268 (LP)			

Chapter 22: Fringe History
Much of history continues to occur in the background, behind the headlines, on the fringe of the historical narrative.

Date	Day	Assignment	Due Date	✓	Grade
Week 4	Day 106	Read **Lesson 1 — Bread** (SB) Answer Discussion Question Page 147 • (LP)			
	Day 107	Read **Lesson 2 — Man's Best Friend** (SB) Answer Discussion Question Page 148 (LP)			
	Day 108	Read **Lesson 3 — Legends** (SB) Answer Discussion Question Page 149 (LP)			
	Day 109	Read **Lesson 4 — The Importance of Paper** (SB) Answer Discussion Question Page 150 (LP)			
	Day 110	Read **Lesson 5 — Dumb Kings** (SB) Answer Discussion Question Page 151 (LP) Optional **Chapter 22 Exam** 1 or 2 Page 269-270 (LP)			

Chapter 23: Early Britain: Island Topography
England's rural areas have never been as populated as they were when the Picts, Scots, Celts, and Britons hunted its wild forests and lonely highlands.

Date	Day	Assignment	Due Date	✓	Grade
Week 5	Day 111	Read **Lesson 1 — A Short History** (SB) Answer Discussion Question Page 153 • (LP)			
	Day 112	Read **Lesson 2 — Secondary Source** (SB) Answer Discussion Question Page 154 (LP)			
	Day 113	Read **Lesson 3 — Normal Invasion** (SB) Answer Discussion Question Page 155 (LP)			
	Day 114	Read **Lesson 4 — Government and Law: The Magna Carta** (SB) Answer Discussion Question Page 156 (LP)			
	Day 115	Read **Lesson 5 — How Robin Hood Came to be an Outlaw** (SB) Answer Discussion Question Page 157 (LP) Optional **Chapter 23 Exam** 1 or 2 Page 271-272 (LP)			

Chapter 24: Islam: For Allah and Caliph
Never had a religion with such new, untested roots demanded so much from its followers. Allah was not the loving God of the Old and New Testament.

Date	Day	Assignment	Due Date	✓	Grade
Week 6	Day 116	Read **Lesson 1 — Muhammad** (SB) Answer Discussion Question Page 159 • (LP)			
	Day 117	Read **Lesson 2 — Islam Compared to Christianity** (SB) Answer Discussion Question Page 160 (LP)			
	Day 118	Read **Lesson 3 — Militant Islam — One View** (SB) Answer Discussion Question Page 161 (LP)			
	Day 119	Read **Lesson 4 — A Touch of TLC** (SB) Answer Discussion Question Page 162 (LP)			
	Day 120	Read **Lesson 5 — Militant Islam** (SB) Answer Discussion Question Page 163 (LP) Optional **Chapter 24 Exam** 1 or 2 Page 273-274 (LP)			

Chapter 25: Islam Spreads: The Sword of Allah
Allah was not a god to be trifled with. He would ask his people to live in uneasiness with themselves, and to conquer, convert, or kill, all those who were outsiders.

Date	Day	Assignment	Due Date	✓	Grade
Week 7	Day 121	Read **Lesson 1 — The Caliphs** (SB) Answer Discussion Question Page 165 • (LP)			
	Day 122	Read **Lesson 2 — The Islamic Army** (SB) Answer Discussion Question Page 166 (LP)			
	Day 123	Read **Lesson 3 — Abbasids** (SB) Answer Discussion Question Page 167 (LP)			
	Day 124	Read **Lesson 4 — Ottoman Empire** (SB) Answer Discussion Question Page 168 (LP)			
	Day 125	Read **Lesson 5 — Sociology: The Islamic Family** (SB) Answer Discussion Question Page 169 (LP) Optional **Chapter 25 Exam** 1 or 2 Page 275-276 (LP)			

Chapter 26: Ancient Spain: Inferiority Complex
Spain stumbled into Western Europe with a sword and Bible and often forgot which one it had in which hand.

Date	Day	Assignment	Due Date	✓	Grade
Week 8	Day 126	Read **Lesson 1 — Geography: Iberian Peninsula** (SB) Answer Discussion Question Page 171 • (LP)			
	Day 127	Read **Lesson 2 — The History of Spain** (SB) Answer Discussion Question Page 172 (LP)			
	Day 128	Read **Lesson 3 — The Moors in Spain** (SB) Answer Discussion Question Page 173 (LP)			
	Day 129	Read **Lesson 4 — Charles Martel** (SB) Answer Discussion Question Page 174 (LP)			
	Day 130	Read **Lesson 5 — A Historical Essay** (SB) Answer Discussion Question Page 175 (LP) Optional **Chapter 26 Exam** 1 or 2 Page 277-278 (LP)			

Chapter 27: The Middle Ages: A People Under Stress
The Middle Ages was birthed in the smoldering fires of Rome and would end in the smoldering fires of Tenochtitlan.

Date	Day	Assignment	Due Date	✓	Grade
Week 9	Day 131	Read **Lesson 1 — Middle Ages: The Dark Ages?** (SB) Answer Discussion Question Page 177 • (LP)			
	Day 132	Read **Lesson 2 — Knights** (SB) Answer Discussion Question Page 178 (LP)			
	Day 133	Read **Lesson 3 — Primary Source: The Charter of Liberties** (SB) Answer Discussion Question Page 179 (LP)			
	Day 134	Read **Lesson 4 — Feudalism** (SB) Answer Discussion Question Page 180 (LP)			
	Day 135	Read **Lesson 5 — Vikings** (SB) Answer Discussion Question Page 181 (LP) Optional **Chapter 27 Exam** 1 or 2 Page 279-280 (LP)			

Second Semester-Fourth Quarter

Chapter 28: Life in the Middle Ages: Emotive Legends

Medieval life was hard but it also was full of adventure, folklore, and faith. One-third of the year was religious holidays. Medieval man had folk heroes, good King Arthur and generous, magnanimous Robin Hood.

	Day	Assignment			
Week 1	Day 136	Read **Lesson 1 — Medieval Occupations** (SB) Answer Discussion Question Page 183 • (LP)			
	Day 137	Read **Lesson 2 — Medieval Women** (SB) Answer Discussion Question Page 184 (LP)			
	Day 138	Read **Lesson 3 — Paris, France** (SB) Answer Discussion Question Page 185 (LP)			
	Day 139	Read **Lesson 4 — Primary Source Material** (SB) Answer Discussion Question Page 186 (LP)			
	Day 140	Read **Lesson 5 — Medieval Art** (SB) Answer Discussion Question Page 187 (LP) Optional **Chapter 28 Exam** 1 or 2 Page 281-282 (LP)			

Chapter 29: Life In The Middle Ages: Complexity

The Middle Ages ended with the realization that there was a world beyond the Canary Islands and the hope that there might be a shortcut to China. The modern world has not abandoned that Quixotic attitude or something like it in one thousand years.

	Day	Assignment			
Week 2	Day 141	Read **Lesson 1 — Food and Famine** (SB) Answer Discussion Question Page 189 • (LP)			
	Day 142	Read **Lesson 2 — Health** (SB) Answer Discussion Question Page 190 (LP)			
	Day 143	Read **Lesson 3 — Romance** (SB) Answer Discussion Question Page 191 (LP)			
	Day 144	Read **Lesson 4 — Life in a Medieval Castle** (SB) Answer Discussion Question Page 192 (LP)			
	Day 145	Read **Lesson 5 — Peasant Life** (SB) Answer Discussion Question Page 193 (LP) Optional **Chapter 29 Exam** 1 or 2 Page 283-284 (LP)			

Chapter 30: Age of Charlemagne: A Man Creates an Era

Charlemagne was a good modern despot, but his reign presaged many later bad ones.

	Day	Assignment			
Week 3	Day 146	Read **Lesson 1 — Overview** (SB) Answer Discussion Question Page 195 • (LP)			
	Day 147	Read **Lesson 2 — The Holy Roman Empire** (SB) Answer Discussion Question Page 196 (LP)			
	Day 148	Read **Lesson 3 — Education** (SB) Answer Discussion Question Page 197 (LP)			
	Day 149	Read **Lesson 4 — Primary Source: The Life of Charlemagne** (SB) Answer Discussion Question Page 198 (LP)			
	Day 150	Read **Lesson 5 — Why Study History ... Primary Sources** (SB) Answer Discussion Question Page 199 (LP) Optional **Chapter 30 Exam** 1 or 2 Page 285-286 (LP)			

Chapter 31: Church Life in the Middle Ages

The Medieval Church, like the Church in all time, is easily caricatured, and universally misunderstood. But it stands in the gap, time and time again, between ignorance and enlightenment, between hope and hopelessness. For a moment — and for the first time, but not for the last time — the world looked into the abyss without holding the hand of God. Surely the Church cannot be blamed for this.

Week 4	Day 151	Read **Lesson 1 — The Early Medieval Papacy** (SB) Answer Discussion Question Page 201 • (LP)			
	Day 152	Read **Lesson 2 — Missionary Activities of the Church** (SB) Answer Discussion Question Page 202 (LP)			
	Day 153	Read **Lesson 3 — Preservation of Learning** (SB) Answer Discussion Question Page 203 (LP)			
	Day 154	Read **Lesson 4 — Cathedrals** (SB) Answer Discussion Question Page 204 (LP)			
	Day 155	Read **Lesson 5 — Men of God** (SB) Answer Discussion Question Page 205 (LP) Optional **Chapter 31 Exam** 1 or 2 Page 287-288 (LP)			

Chapter 32: Medieval Saints: History Makers

These five saints will not be mentioned in most history books, but they surely made more history than all the kings and princes combined. This was to be the beginning of an anonymous hall of fame of world changers, to whose rank the author fervently hopes we all join.

Week 5	Day 156	Read **Lesson 1 — Francis of Assisi** (SB) Answer Discussion Question Page 207 • (LP)			
	Day 157	Read **Lesson 2 — Mechtild of Magdeburg** (SB) Answer Discussion Question Page 208 (LP)			
	Day 158	Read **Lesson 3 — Catherine of Siena** (SB) Answer Discussion Question Page 209 (LP)			
	Day 159	Read **Lesson 4 — Julian of Norwich** (SB) Answer Discussion Question Page 210 (LP)			
	Day 160	Read **Lesson 5 — Ignatius** (SB) Answer Discussion Question Page 211 (LP) Optional **Chapter 32 Exam** 1 or 2 Page 289-290 (LP)			

Chapter 33: The Crusades: Changing World History

The Crusades, the first Holy Wars, infused western Europe with a world vision it would find insinuated into the 21st century.

Week 6	Day 161	Read **Lesson 1 — Overview** (SB) Answer Discussion Question Page 213 • (LP)			
	Day 162	Read **Lesson 2 — The Holy Grail** (SB) Answer Discussion Question Page 214 (LP)			
	Day 163	Read **Lesson 3 — *Heroes of Myth and Legend*** (SB) Answer Discussion Question Page 215 (LP)			
	Day 164	Read **Lesson 4 — The Teutonic Order** (SB) Answer Discussion Question Page 216 (LP)			
	Day 165	Read **Lesson 5 — Consequences and Conclusion** (SB) Answer Discussion Question Page 217 (LP) Optional **Chapter 33 Exam** 1 or 2 Page 291-292 (LP)			

Chapter 34: 1492: The New World

The world in 1492 was as engaging and amazing to Christopher Columbus and his contemporaries as the Garden of Eden was to Adam and Eve the first time they walked among its gardens and rivers.

Date	Day	Assignment	Due Date	✓	Grade
Week 7	Day 166	Read **Lesson 1 — Ferdinand and Isabella** (SB) Answer Discussion Question Page 219 • (LP)			
	Day 167	Read **Lesson 2 — The World in 1492** (SB) Answer Discussion Question Page 220 (LP)			
	Day 168	Read **Lesson 3 — Christopher Columbus** (SB) Answer Discussion Question Page 221 (LP)			
	Day 169	Read **Lesson 4 — Contemporary Account** (SB) Answer Discussion Question Page 222 (LP)			
	Day 170	Read **Lesson 5 — Summary** (SB) Answer Discussion Question Page 223 (LP) Optional **Chapter 34 Exam** 1 or 2 Page 293-294 (LP)			
		Semester Grade			

Daily Worksheets

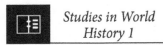
Discussion Questions:

Read Genesis chapter 1 and contemplate how God took a barren void and filled it with life, preparing Earth to be the homeplace of humanity. What astonishes you most about God's special relationship with people from the very beginning?

Discussion Questions:

Identify the following map locations:

_____ Babylon

_____ Euphrates

_____ Tigris

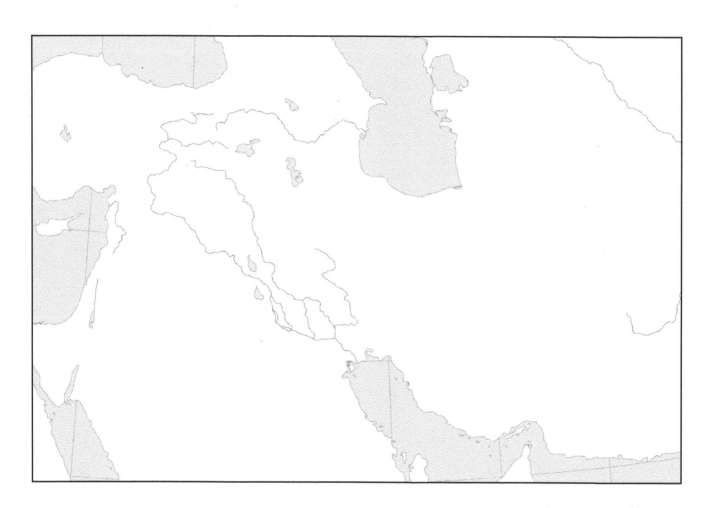

Discussion Questions:

Societies can have two types of laws: written and unwritten. Make a list of the written laws of your home or school and a list of the unwritten laws. For example, lying is a written law code violation, whereas playing soccer before finishing your homework might be a violation of an unwritten law.

Discussion Questions:

Psalm 126 is an agrarian song. King David, or an Israelite, farmer who is talking about both the joy and the sadness of planting time, writes it.

Who is the primary speaker in this verse? What is his vocation? What is his relationship with God?

The farmer saved seed grain through the winter. He often had to watch family members starve — but he dare not use the seed grain. If he did, there would be no crops the next year and all would starve. What observation and conclusion does he draw from this long winter of sacrifice?

What application can you make to your own life?

Discussion Questions:

Contrast the God of the Old Testament with the gods that the Mesopotamians served.

God of the Old Testament	Mesopotamian gods

Discussion Questions:

Historian Jason Thompson in his book *A History of Egypt* argues that few if any other countries have as many threads of continuity running through their entire historical experience, as does Egypt. Speculate upon what affect this common history and stability has had on Egyptian history.

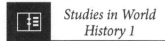
Discussion Questions:

The Nile River Civilization (Egypt) is a land of contrasts. That is especially true as far as the geography goes. Explain.

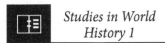

Discussion Questions:

What distinct advantages does a pharaoh-type government bring to a growing, thriving state/empire? What disadvantages?

Discussion Questions:

Retell the Exodus story from the perspective of Ramses II.

Discussion Questions:

Egyptian civilization gave women, at least in the wealthier families, some power. Nefertiti, queen of Egypt, had considerable power and influence. Mesopotamia had no queens. However, Egyptian women were not generally valued. An ancient Egyptian scribe (scholar) noted, "Love your wife . . . but keep her at home and master her." Contrast this view with Jewish, and later, Christian, views of women.

Egyptian view of women	Jewish view of women	Christian view of women

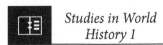
Discussion Questions:

Despite the fact that the land was/is occupied by Islamic Palestinians, why does Israel claim the present-day geographical land on which it is established? Is it a rightful claim?

Discussion Questions:

Define "nomadic food-gatherer" and contrast him with a farmer/agrarian.

Discussion Questions:

Golda Meir, born in Kiev, Russia, became the fourth prime minister of Israel. She and her husband emigrated from the United States to Palestine as Zionists. When Israel won independence, Golda Meir was the only woman in the first Israeli cabinet. She was prime minister from 1969 to 1974. She once said, "Let me tell you something that we Israelis have against Moses. He took us 40 years through the desert in order to bring us to the one spot in the Middle East that has no oil!" Perhaps, though oil was recently found in Israel! Israel has other geographical assets. What are they?

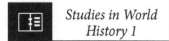

Discussion Questions:

Trace the evolution of government in Israel from the time of Adam's fall to the Roman Empire.

Discussion Questions:

Do you agree with Rabbi Anteby's conclusions?

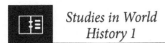

Discussion Questions:

What interesting new development occurred in early Indus civilizations?

Discussion Questions:

How did Hindi priests originate?

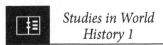

Discussion Questions:

Why was the Gupta Age called the "Golden Age" of India?

Discussion Questions:

Who originated the caste system and which castes existed?

Discussion Questions:

Which Hindi cultural elements does the *Panchatantra* tale exhibit?

Discussion Questions:

Egypt, Mesopotamia, and Israel all developed with a clear sense that they existed as a nation among nations; they had no sense of being isolated. On the contrary, in the case of Israel, the nation was constantly being conquered and subjugated by conquering armies — it could have stood a little isolation! The huge mountain ranges; long, wide, rivers; endless plains; and vast distances between hospitable regions caused the Chinese to develop separately from other civilizations. Surprisingly, however, isolated China was significantly more technologically advanced than the other nations. Why?

Discussion Questions:

Based upon today's reading (you do not have to consult other sources), why do you suppose that the difference among Chinese classes was more pronounced than that of other ancient civilizations?

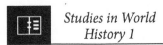

Discussion Questions:

Chinese emperors were able to maintain order even when they had smaller numbers of troops than their opponents. How was this possible?

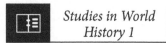

Discussion Questions:

Why were the Chinese uninterested in European trades?

Discussion Questions:

What humiliating practices were inflicted on ancient Chinese women?

Discussion Questions:

Perhaps no empire was so dependent upon a personality or historical figure as the Mongol Empire was dependent upon Genghis Kahn. Why was he such a successful Mongol leader?

Discussion Questions:

Why did the Mongol Empire collapse after only one generation?

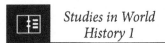
Discussion Questions:

During the early years of World War II, through superior leadership and equipment, the German army was able to obtain one victory after another. The German Panzer tank, for instance, was superior to the American Sherman tank. Nonetheless, the Americans ultimately won the war and the Mongols lost control of China. Why were the Mongols' superior tactics, personnel, and technology able to bring initial victory but unable to sustain long-term control of conquered territories?

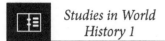

Discussion Questions:

Why did the Mongols choose a nomadic lifestyle when it was unnecessary?

Discussion Questions:

Why did the Mongol confederations eventually destroy Mongol hegemony (political control) over Asia?

Discussion Questions:

In some ways Japan has gained its' identify from what it is not, rather than what it is. It sought to separate itself from all of Asia and to set its destiny in a unique direction, yet this was impossible. Starting in A.D. 600, Japan copied everything Chinese; languages, art, religion — all were copied from China. What unique worldviews did Japan contribute to world history?

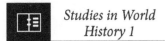
Discussion Questions:

Unlike most ancient empires, Japan resisted expanding its empire until the 19th century. Why?

Discussion Questions:

Why was Japan one of the first civilizations to experience a deficit economy? What was the outcome? What was the solution?

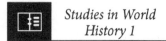
Discussion Questions:

An advance in technology, in most civilizations, is enthusiastically embraced, no matter the consequences. This does not always bring laudable results. The single-family automobile, for instance, popular for the first time in the 1920s, increased mobility but also increased illegitimate births and deaths among juveniles (due to traffic accidents). The Japanese actually said no to one technological advance. What was it? Why?

Discussion Questions:

The Japanese practiced one of the earliest examples of isolationism. What advantages and disadvantages does this policy bring?

Discussion Questions:

Contrast Christianity and Zoroastrianism.

Christianity	Zoroastrianism

Discussion Questions:

How can a religion not believe in any God?

Discussion Questions:

To Buddhism, which is a sort of atheism, "salvation" comes through a heightened, increased degree of knowledge. Why is such a view completely unacceptable to Christians?

Discussion Questions:

Taoism is very popular among "back to nature" movements who celebrate "natural" life unencumbered by the structures of society. This sounds nice, but why would Christians have a problem with this religion?

Discussion Questions:

While Dr. Stobaugh was visiting India in 1987 he wrote an article on Hinduism where he stated, "The Hindus have three million gods but not one savior." What did he mean?

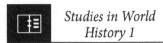

Discussion Questions:

Who were the Minoans and what were their distinctive characteristics?

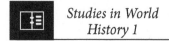
Discussion Questions:

What effect did the geography have on the political development of Greece?

Discussion Questions:

Both Troy and the Battle of Troy existed. However, over the years legends have been added to this historical event. Give an example from your own life where a true event, through exaggeration and embellishment, became something more than the actual event.

Discussion Questions:

Both ancient and modern writers have used the Battle of Thermopylae as an example of the power of a patriotic army defending native soil. The performance of the defenders at the battle of Thermopylae is also used as an example of the advantages of training, equipment, and good use of terrain as force multipliers and has become a symbol of courage against overwhelming odds. What other examples in warfare or other arenas (e.g., sports) can you offer in comparison to the heroic stand of the 300?

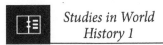

Discussion Questions:

In spite of the fact that democracy seemed to work so well for Athens during the Age of Pericles, why did it take so long — 2,000 years — for it to reappear as a nation state?

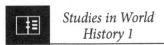
Discussion Questions:

Greek art symbolized humanism — the glorification of man as the most important creature in the universe. The Greeks were the first — and only — ancient culture to be so humanistic. In fact, this pervasive humanism would not return to world history for 3,600 years (with the advent of the Renaissance). Why did the Greeks glorify the human body and why was such a view unpopular in culture? Do not consult any other source. Based on the above discussion, hypothesize as to why this is true.

Discussion Questions:

In what way does Greek drama remain religious?

Discussion Questions:

Compare and contrast Greek and American drama.

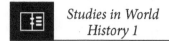
Discussion Questions:

According to Hamilton, why was Euripides unpopular with Athenian viewers?

Discussion Questions:

What were the three periods of Greek sculpture and what distinguished each period?

Discussion Questions:

Describe Alexander's childhood and how/if this childhood gave a hint of what was to come.

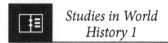
Discussion Questions:

How did Alexander administrate his empire?

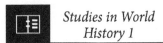
Discussion Questions:

What was Alexander's most important legacy?

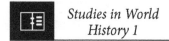

Discussion Questions:

Summarize Professor Worthington's argument. Do you agree, or disagree with him? Why?

Discussion Questions:

If you could fill a library with the most important books ever written, what would be your top ten choices?

1.

2.

3.

4.

5.

6.

7.

8.

9.

10.

Discussion Questions:

From today's reading, predict what the future would be between the Etruscans and the Greeks.

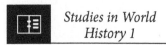
Discussion Questions:

Why would a perfectly good, successful republic reject democracy for autocratic rule?

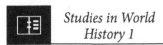
Discussion Questions:

Some contemporary scholars warn that civilizations that accept all religions can easily become intolerant of one religion that claims authenticity. Explain.

Discussion Questions:

Describe what it was like to be a Roman young person.

Discussion Questions:

In spite of the fact that Rome was the most sophisticated and advanced civilization until modern times, the farmer remained the most important citizen in Rome. Why?

Discussion Questions:

In spite of the fact that Rome was the most sophisticated and advanced civilization until modern times, the farmer remained the most important citizen in Rome. Why?

Discussion Questions:

What distinctive traits did Christianity bring to the religious world in AD 50?

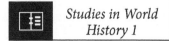
Discussion Questions:

Describe what it was like to be a 13- or 14-year-old young person in the Middle East during the first century A.D.

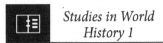
Discussion Questions:

Describe a typical early church service.

Discussion Questions:

Contrast the life of a contemporary Christian with the life of a first-century Christian.

Contemporary Christian	First-century Christian

Discussion Questions:

What is the biblical way for Christians to respond to persecution?

Discussion Questions:

Why were Christian women so valuable to early Church growth?

Discussion Questions:

Why was Christian evangelism so effective in the early Church?

Discussion Questions:

Discuss three early heresies. In your discussion, explain what kernel of truth was in each heresy.

1.

2.

3.

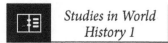

Discussion Questions:

Why did the Bible develop relatively late in early Church history?

Discussion Questions:

What was the allure of Monasticism? Why, suddenly, in the third century, did so many Christians flee to the desert to walk with God?

Discussion Questions:

Why was the Manichaean faith so appealing to the intellectual Augustine? What contemporary worldview temptations exist?

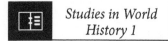
Discussion Questions:

Trace Augustine's spiritual journey to Christ.

Discussion Questions:

By the fourth century, the Church no longer met in homes but met in church buildings and was increasingly controlled by a tertiary ecclesiological government (i.e., the Roman Catholic Church). What advantages and disadvantages did this offer the early Church?

Discussion Questions:

Were the Donatists correct in arguing that recalcitrant, unfaithful believers should not be readmitted into the Church even with extensive penance and repentance?

Discussion Questions:

How can Christians prosper in this post-Christian era?

		Chapter 15 Lesson 5		Name

Discussion Questions:

How can Christians prosper in this post-Christian era?

Discussion Questions:

How were African kingdoms different from other ancient civilizations?

Discussion Questions:

What are some unique features of the Ghanaian kingdom?

Discussion Questions:

Summarize the Ghanaian economy and why it had such a profound impact on African history.

Discussion Questions:

Some historians argue that Mali conquered Ghana by doing what Ghana did "better." Explain.

Discussion Questions:

While Rome, London, and Paris, were insignificant, inhospitable cities in the 12th century, Timbuktu was a thriving, modern, wealthy city full of gold, libraries, and opportunities. However, most Western history books hardly mention it. Why?

Discussion Questions:

Explain why early North American natives were "semi-nomads."

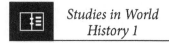
Discussion Questions:

While Central and South American Native American cities, prospered into the 16th century, North American Native American cities disappeared before the end of the 13th century. Why?

Discussion Questions:

Based on today's reading, if you were a Native American, which native group would you prefer?

Discussion Questions:

What effect did kinship have on Native American societies?

Discussion Questions:

In what ways did the horse transform Native American culture?

Discussion Questions:

Describe the topography of South America.

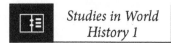
Discussion Questions:

What effect did isolationism have on South American Native American culture?

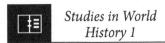
Discussion Questions:

How did animism conflict with western Christianity?

Discussion Questions:

What happened to the Maya?

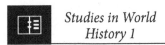

Discussion Questions:

In what ways did the mountainous topography of the Andes affect the Inca Civilization?

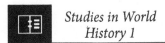
Discussion Questions:

The English historian Edward Gibbon stated that the Byzantium Empire experienced 1,000 years of constant decline. Disagree with Gibbon and explain what really happened.

Discussion Questions:

Why was Justinian such an effective leader?

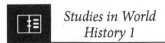
Discussion Questions:

Why is the Bosporus Strait so strategically important?

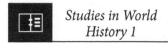
Discussion Questions:

Why did the Eastern and Western Churches separate in A.D. 1054?

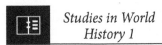
Discussion Questions:

What impact did the Black Death have on world history?

Students in World
History I

Day 95

Chapter 19
Lesson 5

Name

Discussion Questions

What impact did the Black Death have on world history?

Discussion Questions:

Why did the Kievan Russians prosper so quickly after A.D. 500?

Discussion Questions:

Why was the Tatar invasion a good thing for Russia?

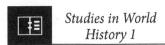

Discussion Questions:

What advantages and disadvantages did the Russian vastness bring to its history?

Discussion Questions:

The author of the Chronicle discusses historical events in the context of Christian theology. What dangers result from such an interpretation?

Discussion Questions:

Trace the history of Moscow's evolution as capital of Russia.

Discussion Questions:

The Balkans have always been a place of turmoil and warfare. From the above discussion, offer some explanations about why this is so.

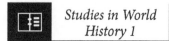
Discussion Questions:

From Tacitus' observations, what can we conclude about Germanic families, government, and warfare?

Discussion Questions:

Why were the Huns so feared in eastern Europe?

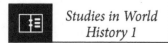

Discussion Questions:

Attila showed much discipline by refusing completely to destroy his Roman enemies. Why?

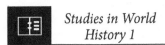
Discussion Questions:

Who were the Cossacks and why did they have such an impact on world history?

Discussion Questions:

What are some things that bread symbolizes in history?

1.

2.

3.

Discussion Questions:

From today's reading, how were dogs used in warfare?

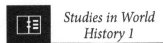
Discussion Questions:

Based on today's reading, which of the legends circulating today are surely false?

Discussion Questions:

How did the battle among animal skins, papyrus, parchment, and paper as a medium for writing and sharing text turn out?

Discussion Questions:

When in world history would illiteracy perhaps be a distinct advantage?

Day 10	Chapter 12 Lesson 5	Name

Discussion Questions:

When in world history would illiteracy perhaps be a distinct advantage?

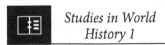
Discussion Questions:

Give a summary of English history until the departure of the Romans.

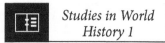

Discussion Questions:

What does Chesterton mean when he says, "Rome itself, which had made all that strong world, was the weakest thing in it. The centre had been growing fainter and fainter, and now the centre disappeared. Rome had as much freed the world as ruled it, and now she could rule no more"?

Discussion Questions:

Why was the *Domesday Book* so important to English history?

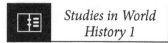
Discussion Questions:

Why was the Magna Carta so important in English history?

Discussion Questions:

The Robin Hood legend, while fictional, is based on fact. There was a historical character somewhat like the legendary figure Robin Hood. Regardless, what does this legend tell us about the values that medieval England cherished?

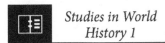
Discussion Questions:

What do you know of Muhammad from things you have read, the media, or what others have said?

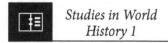

Discussion Questions:

What is your view concerning Islam in America?

Discussion Questions:

Summarize Olasky's arguments.

Discussion Questions:

Do you agree with Ms. Carter's assessment of militant Islam? Will these efforts bring world peace?

Discussion Questions:

What are the roots of Islamic militancy?

Discussion Questions:

Discuss the genesis of the Sunni and Shiites.

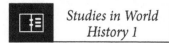

Discussion Questions:

Why was the Islamic Army such a formidable enemy?

Discussion Questions:

Who were the Abbasid and what contributions to world culture did they make?

Discussion Questions:

Both the Umayyad and the Ottoman were able to make significant territory acquisitions in Europe for Islam. Yet, the Ottoman campaigns were very different from the Umayyad. How?

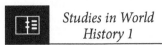
Discussion Questions:

In what ways were Islamic families different from Christian families?

Discussion Questions:

In what ways did Spanish geography affect Spanish history?

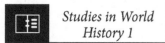
Discussion Questions:

Why did Spain emerge, at the end of the 17th century, as a second-rate European power?

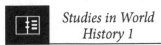
Discussion Questions:

Who were the Moors and what impact did they have on European history?

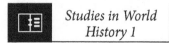

Discussion Questions:

Martel was able to stop the Moors from conquering western Europe. What if the Moors were not stopped and they did indeed conquer western Europe?

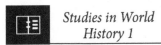

Discussion Questions:

Offer evidence that the author is obviously anti-Roman Catholic.

Discussion Questions:

Were the Middle Ages the "Dark Ages"? Why or why not?

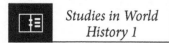

Discussion Questions:

Why were knights a key element of medieval society?

Discussion Questions:

Based on today's reading, nothing like this document appeared in Islamic countries, nor in the Far East. Why?

Discussion Questions:

What advantages and disadvantages did feudalism bring to the medieval world? Is there a better societal structure that would have worked better?

Advantages to feudalism	Disadvantages to feudalism

Discussion Questions:

Write a 300-word, fictional narrative describing a Viking attack. Write the narrative from the perspective of a young person in the community that was attacked.

Discussion Questions:

Write a 300-word, fictional narrative describing a Viking attack. Write the narrative from the perspective of a young person in the community that was attacked.

Discussion Questions:

If you had to choose one medieval occupation, which would you choose? Why?

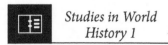

Discussion Questions:

Contrast medieval European women with women in Mesopotamia, Greece, India, and China, places you have studied earlier this year.

Discussion Questions:

Why were European cities fortified?

Discussion Questions:

Pretend that you are a social historian. Based on this document alone, what can you say about medieval life?

Discussion Questions:

In the midst of such traumatic change, the arts flourished in medieval Europe. Why?

Discussion Questions:

What would a typical medieval family eat for breakfast, lunch, and dinner?

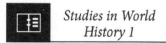

Discussion Questions:

What medieval remedies would be proposed to cure bronchitis?

Discussion Questions:

What caused the rise of courtly love in medieval society?

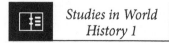
Discussion Questions:

Describe a typical day in a castle.

Discussion Questions:

Discuss the life of a peasant.

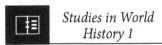
Discussion Questions:

Summarize some of the accomplishments of the reign of Charlemagne.

Discussion Questions:

Why was the Holy Roman Empire created and what advantages and potential problems did it bring?

Discussion Questions:

Compare medieval education to earlier Greek and Roman education. Which would you prefer? Why?

Medieval education	Early Greek education	Roman education

Discussion Questions:

Based on Einhard's description of Charlemagne, describe Charlemagne's Christian life.

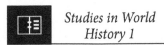
Discussion Questions:

According to Robinson, what advantages do primary sources bring to historical studies?

Discussion Questions:

How did the Roman Catholic Church become so powerful during the Middle Ages?

Discussion Questions:

If you were a pope in the Middle Ages, what sort of missionary strategy would you develop?

Discussion Questions:

Why were all scholarship and learning so important to the medieval church?

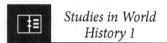

Discussion Questions:

Why were cathedrals, even in poor areas, built with such care and great expense?

Discussion Questions:

Compare the role of medieval clergy with that of modern clergy.

Medieval clergy	Modern clergy

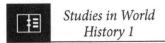

Discussion Questions:

What does Francis mean when he says, "It is in pardoning that we are pardoned"?

Discussion Questions:

What does Mechtild mean in these lines?

> How God Answers the Soul:
>
> It is my nature that makes me love you often,
>
> For I am love itself.
>
> It is my longing that makes me love you intensely,
>
> For I yearn to be loved from the heart.
>
> It is my eternity that makes me love you long,
>
> For I have no end.

Discussion Questions:

Catherine states that "when she was lifted up in prayer, with great elevation of mind, God was not wont to conceal, from the eye of her intellect, the love which He had for His servants, but rather to manifest it." What does Catherine mean? What is she arguing?

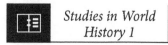

Discussion Questions:

To Julian the supernatural was natural, the presence of God normal. She lived there, so to speak, and walked and talked with God. Are you comfortable with God's supernatural presence in your life? Why or why not?

Discussion Questions:

Ignatius called his Jesuit priesthood to a committed life of constant meditation and hard work. This was a winsome combination.

Discussion Questions:

What were the causes of the Crusades?

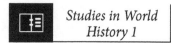

Discussion Questions:

Was there really a Holy Grail?

Discussion Questions:

What does this legend about the Holy Grail tell the reader about what medieval audiences preferred in heroes?

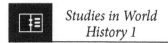
Discussion Questions:

What dangers ultimately occur when a mercenary, warlike organization allies itself with the Church?

Discussion Questions:

How did the Crusades change world history?

Discussion Questions:

Why did Spain show such interest in overseas exploration?

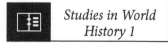

Discussion Questions:

Describe Native American building projects in North American.

Discussion Questions:

Why did Columbus sail west to reach the East Indies? Why did that seem logical?

Discussion Questions:

Columbus reports on his voyage to King Ferdinand and Queen Isabella of Spain:

> These people in the Caribbean have no creed and they are not idolaters, but they are very gentle and do not know what it is to be wicked, or to kill others, or to steal . . . and they are sure that we come from Heaven. . . . So your Highnesses should resolve to make them Christians, for I believe that if you begin, in a little while you will achieve the conversion of a great number of peoples to our holy faith, with the acquisition of great lordships and riches and all their inhabitants for Spain. For without doubt there is a very great amount of gold in these lands. . . .

> The people of this island [Hispaniola], and of all the others that I have found and seen ... have no iron or steel, nor any weapons. . . . They have no other weapons than the stems of reeds . . . on the end of which they fix little sharpened stakes. Even these they dare not use. . . . they are incurably timid. . .

> I have not found, nor had any information of monsters, except of an island which is here the second in the approach of the Indies, which is inhabited by a people whom, in all the islands, they regard as very ferocious, who eat human flesh. . . .

> They brought us parrots and balls of cotton and spears and many other things, which they exchanged for the glass beads and hawks' bells. They willingly traded everything they owned. They do not bear arms, and do not know them, for I showed them a sword, they took it by the edge and cut themselves out of ignorance. With fifty men we could subjugate them all and make them do whatever we want.

Why, according to Columbus, should Spain be interested in the New World?

Discussion Questions:

Who was Columbus? A self-seeking opportunist? Or a sincere believer trying to advance the Kingdom of God on earth as it is in heaven?

Chapter Exam Section

Fill in the blanks with words from the following list:

Agrarian Societies   Mesopotamia

Antediluvian   Monotheism

Civilization   Nomadic Societies

Hammurabi Code   Polytheism

Marduk   Sumer

1. _____ A highly developed, sustaining society.

2. _____ Time before the Great Flood.

3. _____ The area approximately between and around the Tigris and Euphrates Rivers.

4. _____ The first significant civilization group in Mesopotamia.

5. _____ The first written rule of law in the world.

6. _____ People groups whose main livelihood is farming.

7. _____ People groups whose main livelihood is farming.

8. _____ A religion that worships one god.

9. _____ A religion that worships many gods.

10. _____ A significant Babylonian god.

Short Answer Essay:

You are an early Mesopotamian village leader. You are responsible to find a location to build your village. Based upon this map, where would you recommend? Why?

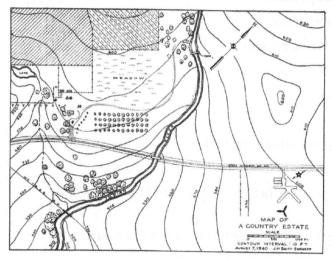

Fill in the blanks with words from the following list:

Black Land   Old Kingdom

Delta   Oligarchy

Despot   Pharaoh

Middle Kingdom   Red Land

New Kingdom   Totalitarian

1. _____ Arising after the Great Flood, developed a strong national government — the first in history.

2. _____ There were several civil wars and King Mentuhotep II united the Kingdom again but he moved the capital to Thebes.

3. _____ It was during this time, probably during the reign of Ramses II, that Moses took his people from Egypt to the Promised Land.

4. _____ Lowlands near the mouth of a river.

5. _____ Fertile loam soil.

6. _____ Arid, dry land, usually rich in iron ore.

7. _____ A king/leader of Egypt.

8. _____ A government whose leadership is one strong leader.

9. _____ Tertiary, omnipotent, usually malevolent leader.

10. _____ A government where total control is lodged in one leader.

Short Answer Essay:

Religion, even bad, wrong religion, creates vital, long-lasting civilizations. For instance, Islam has produced some of the most enduring civilizations in world history. Egypt was very religious. They built pyramids to house the mummified bodies of the pharaohs until they returned to reclaim their corpus beings. Yet, perhaps no religion has more to do with its establishment and maintenance than Christianity. Why has Christianity so successfully encouraged civilization building?

Fill in the blanks with words from the following list:

Abraham	Judges
Canaan	Judicial, Legislative, Executive
Diaspora	Kubbutzim
Exodus	Wadis
Israel	Zionist

1. _____ The father patriarch of Judaism.

2. _____ Another name for Jacob, the name of the Jewish state.

3. _____ The Promised Land, the land promised to the Jewish people.

4. _____ The liberation of the Jewish people from bondage in Egypt.

5. _____ After the destruction of the Temple (AD 70), the Jewish people spread all over the world.

6. _____ Radical Jewish thought that wishes to form a Jewish state.

7. _____ Communal living groups in Israel.

8. _____ Mainly dry water courses.

9. _____ Leaders of Israel during a period of great stress in Israeli history.

10. _____ Three different branches of government.

Short Answer Essay:

In *The Case for Peace*, American Jewish lawyer Alan Dershowitz identifies twelve geopolitical barriers to peace between Israel and Palestine — and explains how to move around them and push the process forward. According to Dershowitz, achieving a lasting peace will require more than tough-minded negotiations between Israelis and Palestinians. Surveying this outpouring of vilification, Dershowitz deconstructs the smear tactics used by Israel-haters and shows how this kind of anti-Israel rhetoric is the main obstacle to overcome for peace to come. Do you agree?

Fill in the blanks with words from the following list:

Castes   *Panchatantra*

Gandharva Vivaha   Polytheists

Guru   Ramayana

Harrappan   Saris

Marketplace   Vedas

1. _____ First people group to reach India.
2. _____ Place where commerce occurs.
3. _____ Hindu sacred texts.
4. _____ Religion that worships many gods.
5. _____ An ancient Hindu Sanskrit epic.
6. _____ Ancient Indian beast fables.
7. _____ Religious teacher.
8. _____ Love marriage.
9. _____ Woman's garment.
10. _____ Hindu social class.

Short Answer Essay:

By this time you have studied the genesis of the Mesopotamian, Egyptian, and Indus civilizations. Based on your readings in this text only, which one originated first? Why?

Fill in the blanks with words from the following list:

Calligraphy   Galloping Horse Ships

Class System   Mandarins

Confucius   Oriental Monarch

Conscripted   Yellow River

Feudal System   Zhing He

1. _____ The Huang He, formerly known as the Hwang Ho, is the second-longest river in China. It is the location of many ancient Chinese people groups.

2. _____ Division among people groups according to special criteria.

3. _____ An Eastern autocrat, monarch, who is usually more despotic than Western types.

4. _____ Early Chinese philosopher.

5. _____ Decorative writing.

6. _____ A Chinese people type.

7. _____ Forced to serve for a purpose.

8. _____ Hierarchical system based on patronage.

9. _____ Famous Chinese naval captain.

10. _____ Description of massive Chinese vessels.

Short Answer Essay:

Historian Daniel Boorstin writes, "The Chinese would not establish their own permanent bases within the tributary states, but instead hoped to make 'the whole world' into voluntary admirers of the one and only center of civilization. With this in mind, the Chinese navy dared not loot the states that it visited. Zheng He would not seek slaves or gold or silver or spices. Nothing would suggest that the Chinese needed what other nations had." Compare this view with European exploration and colonization efforts in the 1500s.

Fill in the blanks with words from the following list:

Confederation	Kublai Khan
Domesticated Animals	Labor Intensive
Empire	Marco Polo
Genghis Khan	Mongol
Khan	Tatars

1. _____ Lands ruled by single authority.

2. _____ People group coming from the Mongolian Steppes, conquered China.

3. _____ Central Asian warlike people; absorbed by Mongols.

4. _____ Mongol chief.

5. _____ First major leader of the Mongols.

6. _____ Greatest Mongol chief, grandson of Genghis Kahn.

7. _____ Italian explorer who opened up trade with China.

8. _____ As opposed to wild animals.

9. _____ An economy that is based on large numbers of labor workers.

10. _____ A loose government composed of voluntary consenting states.

Short Answer Essay:

What is the legacy of the Mongol Empire?

Fill in the blanks with words from the following list:

Bakufu

Commodore Matthew Perry

Daimyo

Guilds

Japanese Feudalism

Meiji Period

Sakoku

Shoguns

Tertiary Leaders

Tokugawa Period

1. _____ Japanese feudal lord.
2. _____ Shogun commander.
3. _____ Important period of Japanese history where Japan was ruled by shoguns.
4. _____ A Japanese era which extended from September 1868 through July 1912.
5. _____ Japanese leader.
6. _____ Leaders who are important, but not at the center of the action.
7. _____ Japanese hierarchical government based on patronage.
8. _____ Professional organizations.
9. _____ Foreign relations policy that forbid outsiders from entering Japan.
10. _____ The American who opened trade to China.

Short Answer Essay:

Much that is distinctive in Japanese culture has resulted from geographic factors, which provided harsh challenges but maximum national security. An isolated island, however wonderful, insures some limits that can be debilitative. In Japan, location was the most important early enculturation factor; approximately 200 miles of water separated the highly populated islands from the mainland. Nonetheless, isolated as they were during their early history, the Japanese were comfortable enough to experiment with new ways while retaining a deep attachment to their land and its traditional culture. The Egyptians enjoyed some isolation too. Compare these two, relatively, isolated civilizations.

Fill in the blanks with words from the following list:

Atheism

Avesta

Conversion

Hinduism

Humanism

Laozi

Meditation

Omnipotent

Omniscient

Wu Wei

1. _____ Divinely present everywhere.

2. _____ Divinely in control everywhere.

3. _____ Sacred texts of Zoroastrianism.

4. _____ Total change to a new status or allegiance.

5. _____ A philosophy that places mankind at the center of the discussion.

6. _____ A belief that there is no god.

7. _____ To reflect on life and truth.

8. _____ A concept of Taoism: knowing when to act and when not to act.

9. _____ The founder of Taoism.

10. _____ A polytheistic, animistic religion.

Short Answer Essay:

Many world religions emerged in times of great stress, or, declination. Why?

Fill in the blanks with words from the following list:

Aeneas

Alexander

Battle of Thermopylae

Democracy

Hellas

Iliad

King Leonidas

Marathon

Mycenaeans

Odyssey

1. _____ Greece.

2. _____ Cultural period in ancient Greece.

3. _____ Homer's epic classic about the siege of Troy.

4. _____ Homer's epic classic about Odysseus' return from Troy.

5. _____ Alexander the Great conquered most of the known world.

6. _____ The founder of Rome, survivor of Troy.

7. _____ Where the Spartan 300 stopped the Persian army for two days.

8. _____ King of the Spartan 300.

9. _____ A Greek messenger ran approximately 26 miles to Athens to tell his superiors that the Persians were defeated. He died afterwards.

10. _____ Government by the people.

Short Answer Essay:

No civilization was affected by geography as much as Greece was affected. Explain.

Fill in the blanks with words from the following list:

Aristotelian Tradition   Motif

Classical   Pathos

Didactic   Poetics

Greek Enlightenment   Renaissance

Hellenistic   Satyr Plays

1. _____ In literature, pathos is the "heart" or "spirit" of a literary work.
2. _____ Classical revival at the end of the Middle Ages.
3. _____ Traditional.
4. _____ Greek.
5. _____ A time of significant artistic production.
6. _____ Greek tragic comedies.
7. _____ Artistic genres that teach a lesson.
8. _____ Tradition of using the Socratic dialogue and the didactic.
9. _____ Aristotle's book discussing poetry.
10. _____ Theme.

Short Answer Essay:

Culture is "The behavior patterns, arts, beliefs, institutions, and all other products of human work and thought, especially as expressed in a particular community or period." Where do we discern culture? In the billboards that line our highways, in the songs that play on our radios, in the movies that play on our theaters. Culture is exemplified in the courses our universities teach, in the books our nation reads. Christian teacher Os Guinness warns us that at some point Americans will become fed up with the excesses and dysfunctional aspects of our culture. He says that as American mainline culture fails to sustain Americans in their hedonistic pursuit of self interest, they will want something more. It is now questionable whether America's cultural order is capable of nourishing the freedom, responsibility, and civility that Americans require to sustain democracy. Modernity (a word to describe modern American culture) creates problems far deeper than drugs. It creates a crisis of cultural authority in which America's beliefs, ideals, and traditions are losing their compelling power in society. William Bennett is right to warn us that there is a "death of outrage" in our country but he might add that there is a numbness spreading across the land that offers much opportunity for Christians in general. Why?

Fill in the blanks with words from the following list:

Alexandria   Origen

Byzantium   Persepolis

Darius III   Pharos Island

Hellenistic   Ptolemy

Octavian   Septuagint

1. _____ The Eastern Roman Empire.

2. _____ Persian King.

3. _____ Persepolis was the ceremonial capital of the Achaemenid Empire (ca. 550–330 BC).

4. _____ Greek in nature.

5. _____ Famous Egyptian/Greek city.

6. _____ Alexander's top general.

7. _____ Island off Alexander. Housed the Pharos light house.

8. _____ Greek version of the Old Testament.

9. _____ The first Roman emperor.

10. _____ Early Church Father.

Short Answer Essay:

Most scholars argue that Alexander the Great was a real "history maker" — someone, who, in his lifetime, changed the course of history. But was he really? What makes a true history maker?

Fill in the blanks with words from the following list:

Etruscans   Republic

Indigenous   Romulus

Julius Caesar   Senate

Phoenicians   Tiber River

Plains of Latium   Utilitarian

1. _____ Local people.

2. _____ Where the Latin people-group originated.

3. _____ River that runs through Rome.

4. _____ The people group who lived in the area of Rome before the Latins invaded.

5. _____ A sea people in the Middle East.

6. _____ A political entity with elected officials.

7. _____ One of the legendary founders of Rome.

8. _____ The legislators of Rome.

9. _____ The last leader of the Republic.

10. _____ Things that are practical and useful.

Short Answer Essay:

In January of 49 BC, Julius Caesar led his army across the Rubicon River in Northern Italy and plunged the Roman Republic into civil war. Caesar's rival, Pompey, fled to Greece. Within three months Caesar controlled the entire Italian peninsula and in Spain had defeated the legions loyal to Pompey. Caesar now pursued Pompey to Greece. Although outnumbered, Caesar crushed the forces of his enemy but not before Pompey escaped to Egypt. Following Pompey to Egypt, Caesar was presented with his rival's severed head as a token of friendship. Before leaving the region, Caesar established Cleopatra as his surrogate ruler of Egypt. Caesar defeated his remaining rivals in North Africa in 47 BC and returned to Rome with his authority firmly established. Caesar continued to consolidate his power and in February 44 BC, he declared himself dictator for life. This act, along with his continual effort to adorn himself with the trappings of power, turned many in the Senate against him (http://www.eyewitnesstohistory. com/caesar2.htm). Sixty members of the Senate concluded that the only resolution to the problem was to assassinate Caesar. Finally, friends, led by Brutus did exactly that — assassinated the new Emperor. Brutus was a good man, and he reluctantly killed his friend. He did this to save the Republic. But were his actions justified?

Fill in the blanks with words from the following list:

Christian Worship Assembly   Gospels

Deacons   Messiah

Didache   Nazareth

Elders   Presbytery

Epistles   Rabbi

1. _____ The Savior of mankind.

2. _____ The town where Jesus lived.

3. _____ Spiritual leader of the Jewish community.

4. _____ A group who serves in the church.

5. _____ Leadership group in the Church.

6. _____ The local church leaders.

7. _____ A term for an early church.

8. _____ Sacred letters in the Church.

9. _____ Matthew, Mark, Luke, and John.

10. _____ Writings about the early church that are not sacred.

Short Answer Essay:

The Body of Christ in the first century was so powerful! The Church conferred every mission, and was guided solely in its choice by the signs given by the Spirit. Christians lived, and some prospered in the Roman state, but few, even when persecuted, chose Rome over Jesus Christ. The Church changed society, not vice versa. Today, church growth has stagnated in some places. Christian behavior, regrettably, seems to be no different from secular behavior. What has happened to the Church and how can we reclaim some of the fervor of the early Church?

Fill in the blanks with words from the following list:

Anabaptists   Mennonite

Apocryphal   Monotheistic

Apologists   Quakers

Canon   Spiritual Gifts

Church Fathers   Systematic Church Dogma

1. _____ Gifts of the Holy Spirit were given to the Church, beginning at Pentecost, for the empowering of the Saints, and as an encouragement and helps.

2. _____ To believe in one God.

3. _____ Defenders of the Christian faith.

4. _____ Comprehensive church doctrine.

5. _____ Historical defenders of the faith.

6. _____ The officially sanctioned books of the Bible.

7. _____ Debatable inter-testament books of the Bible.

8. _____ Early, believer baptism, pacifist sect of Christianity.

9. _____ Believed in believer baptism.

10. _____ Had no clergy and liturgy.

Short Answer Essay:

The early Church had no systematic theology. Jesus more or less wisely kept himself far removed from all metaphysics. He had only one dogma, his own divine Sonship and the divinity of his mission. The whole theology of the primitive Church might be embraced in one line: "Jesus is the Messiah, the Son of God." This belief rested upon a peremptory argument — the fact of the resurrection, of which the disciples claimed to be witnesses. To attest the resurrection of Jesus was the task which all considered as being specially imposed upon them. It was, however, very soon a need for more theology arose. Why?

Fill in the blanks with words from the following list:

Atonement	Exegesis
Barbarians	Hegemony
Cicero	Manichaeanism
Donatism	Pelagianism
Dualistic	Visigoth Alaric

1. _____ Germanic people who conquered the western portion of the Roman Empire.

2. _____ A very popular 5th-century religion among intellectuals.

3. _____ Famous Roman orator.

4. _____ Sacrifice for sins.

5. _____ A view that good and bad are equal in strength.

6. _____ Analysis of Scripture.

7. _____ A sect of people who could not forgive apostate repenting Christians.

8. _____ An emphasis on freewill.

9. _____ Germanic barbarian tribes.

10. _____ Political and cultural control.

Short Answer Essay:

One afternoon, Augustine wrestled anxiously while walking in his garden. Suddenly he heard a child's sing-song voice repeating, "Take up and read." On a table lay a collection of Paul's epistles he'd been reading; he picked it up and read the first thing he saw: "Not in reveling and drunkenness, not in lust and wantonness, not in quarrels and rivalries. Rather, arm yourselves with the Lord Jesus Christ, spend no more thought on nature and nature's appetites" (Rom. 13:13–14). He later wrote, "No further would I read; nor needed I: for instantly at the end of this sentence, by a light as it were of serenity infused into my heart, all the darkness of doubt vanished away." (Christian History)

Describe your own conversion being careful to offer Scriptures that were significant to you and led you to the Lord.

Fill in the blanks with words from the following list:

Commodities	Niger
Ghana	Sahara Desert
The Gold Coast	Songhay
Industrial State	Sundjata
Mauritania	Timbuktu

1. _____ Ancient West African nation.

2. _____ A desert in northwest Africa.

3. _____ Goods and services that have economic value.

4. _____ West African country.

5. _____ Nations whose primary economic prosperity is tied to industries.

6. _____ West African coastline that sold vast amounts of gold to Europeans.

7. _____ An important West African river.

8. _____ Founder of the Mali Empire.

9. _____ Famous African city.

10. _____ A people group who replaced the Malis.

Short Answer Essay:

Compare European civilizations with African civilizations from AD 500 to AD 1500.

Fill in the blanks with words from the following list:

Cahokia Mounds   Mound Building

Deforestation   Native Americans

Domicile   Patrilineal

Kinship   Sedentary

Matrilineal   Shamans

1. _____ Native, indigenous people groups in the Northern hemisphere of the Americas.

2. _____ Native American burial mounds and large hills of dirt built, perhaps, to escape high water.

3. _____ Spectacular mounds in Middle America.

4. _____ Rapid and totally debilitating removal of forests from an area.

5. _____ Native American priests and religious leaders.

6. _____ To find one's identity from one's mother.

7. _____ Hunters-gatherers: These are hunters who live in one place.

8. _____ To build ties and relationships around family ties.

9. _____ Place where one lives.

10. _____ Lineage from the father.

Short Answer Essay:

Agriculture was practiced all over the Americas from the woodlands of eastern North America to the high Andes Mountains in South America. Native Americans cultivated over 100 different crops including peppers, squash, and tomatoes. Some crops, particularly maize, potatoes, and manioc, became essential sources of food to dense populations. As in earlier civilizations, agriculture imposed restrictions on population growth and the patterns of human action; as American societies depended increasingly on agriculture, a series of processes which created complex social systems. Explain.

Fill in the blanks with words from the following list:

Aesthetics	Functionality
Andes Mountains	Glaciers
Bureaucracy	Gypsum
Conquistadors	Machu Pachacutec
Cosmology	Talismans

1. _____ A mountain range through southern South America.
2. _____ Huge layers of ice.
3. _____ Religious charms.
4. _____ Study of the supernatural.
5. _____ White substance/mineral.
6. _____ Operational.
7. _____ Ideas of beauty.
8. _____ Important Inca ruler.
9. _____ Spanish explorers.
10. _____ Administrative system.

Short Answer Essay:

Describe the characteristics of the Olmec people.

Fill in the blanks with words from the following list:

Anti-Semites   Excommunication

Bubonic Plague   Holy Roman Empire

Civil Law   Justinian I

Constantinople   Legal Precedence

Eastern Orthodox Church   Pandemics

1. _____ The Central European Empire.

2. _____ New name of the capital of Byzantium.

3. _____ Most famous and capable Byzantium leader.

4. _____ Civil law procedure enhanced by Justinian reforms.

5. _____ Law relating to property, not criminal activity.

6. _____ A bacterial infection that devastated Europe.

7. _____ The Eastern Catholic Church with a patriarch at Constantinople.

8. _____ To be cast out of the Church and its fellowship.

9. _____ Massive, international outbreaks of disease.

10. _____ People who are prejudiced against Jews.

Short Answer Essay:

The Byzantium Empire was truly the first melting-pot frontier. It was the first modern empire that including several different people groups. The fortunes of the empire thus were intimately entwined with those of peoples whose achievements and failures constitute the medieval history of both Europe and Asia. How did the Byzantium government maintain order is such an ethnically diverse group?

Fill in the blanks with words from the following list:

Caucasus Mountains   Romanov Dynasty
Cossacks   Slavic Tribes
Germanic Tribes   Ural Mountains
Kiev   Vikings
Moscow   Volga Steppes

1. _____ Ancient middle European tribes who settled in Russia.
2. _____ Central European tribes.
3. _____ Rolling hills around the longest river in Europe.
4. _____ The capital of a 400-year Kevan Rus Empire.
5. _____ Central Asian fierce warriors who lived on the steppes.
6. _____ Capital of Romanov Russia.
7. _____ The longest Russian ruling family.
8. _____ Important mountain range in Russia.
9. _____ Mountains in southern Russia.
10. _____ Scandinavian Norsemen who ravaged Europe and Russia.

Short Answer Essay:

In 988 Vladimir, grand prince of Kiev, became a Christian in the Byzantine, or Eastern Orthodox, tradition. Russian ties to Christianity were profound and extensive. Greek missionaries moved into Russia, sharing Christ with many unsaved souls. The missionaries also developed the Cyrillic alphabet. For the next four centuries, Kievan Rus developed into a well-organized, democratic, urban, commercial society. It was the last democratic Russian Republic (of sorts) until the end of the Soviet Regime in 1990. At the height of its glory in the 11th century, Kievan Rus was populated by 7 to 8 million people and included the cities of Kiev, Novgorod, and Smolensk. It was the largest and most populous state in Europe. Yet, virtually no one has heard of it. Why?

Fill in the blanks with words from the following list:

Attila	Huns
Bishop of Margus	Magyars
Bulgars	Ostrogoths
Cossacks	Ukraine
Dacians	Visigoths

1. _____ Powerful barbarian tribe in Eastern Europe.
2. _____ Gothic barbarians.
3. _____ Gothic people who mostly lived in Germany.
4. _____ Gothic people who lived in Czechoslovakia.
5. _____ Ancient Transylvanian people.
6. _____ Ancestors of Bulgaria.
7. _____ Leader of the Huns.
8. _____ Roman bishop who negotiated with Attila.
9. _____ Central Russian province.
10. _____ Fierce warriors who lived in Eastern Europe and southern Russia.

Short Answer Essay:

Ethnic nationalism has been a real problem in Eastern Europe. Without using another resource, define what this term means.

Fill in the blanks with words from the following list:

Archetypal

Charlemagne

King Arthur

Mastiff

Papyrus

Parchment

Passover

Pergamon

Prester John

Robin Hood

1. _____ Jewish religious celebration.
2. _____ A type.
3. _____ A large breed dog.
4. _____ Mythical Briton King.
5. _____ Mythical English hero.
6. _____ Imaginary historical figure.
7. _____ Or Pergamum was a Greek city in Turkey.
8. _____ High quality paper.
9. _____ Paper.
10. _____ Famous Holy Roman Emperor.

Short Answer Essay:

There are two major points of view about the historical process. One says that history is nothing more than a disordered collection of random happenings. Therefore no meaning can be found in history any more than one can find meaning and purpose in the world of nature. The opposite point of view, the majority opinion, asserts that there is a design, purpose, or pattern in history. Which position do you believe to be true?

Fill in the blanks with words from the following list:

Alfred the Great   Constitutional Law

Anglo-Saxons   Domesday Book

Britons   King John

Celts   Magna Carta

Charter of Liberties   Picts

1. _____ Germanic tribe that occupied England.

2. _____ Wild Germanic tribe in Scotland.

3. _____ Indigenous group mix of Britons and Celts.

4. _____ German group that invaded and conquered England.

5. _____ The greatest Anglo-Saxon king.

6. _____ First Norman census of England.

7. _____ Major declaration of the rights of Englishmen.

8. _____ King when Magna Carta was signed.

9. _____ Written and signed by King Henry I after the Magna Carta.

10. _____ Law and legislation based on a written document.

Short Answer Essay:

Discuss the Roman occupation of Britain and its influence on the island.

Fill in the blanks with words from the following list:

9/11	Koran
Abyssinia	Mecca
A.D. 571	Modernity
Bedouin	Muhammad
Islamic Fundamentalism	Wailing Wall

1. _____ Nomads who were food gatherers.
2. _____ The sacred book of Islam.
3. _____ Founder of Islam.
4. _____ Ethiopia.
5. _____ Remaining wall of the destroyed temple.
6. _____ Attack on America by Islamic fundamentalists.
7. _____ Militant Islam.
8. _____ Movement starting in 1900 that posits that science is most important.
9. _____ The date of Muhammad's birth.
10. _____ City near where Muhammad was born.

Short Answer Essay:

Compare the Lord's Prayer to a sacred Islamic prayer, The Fatitha. How are they similar? How are they different?

The Lord's Prayer	The Fatiha
Adoration.	**Adoration.**
(a) Our Father which art in heaven, Hallowed be thy name. Thy Kingdom come.	(a) Praise be to God, Lord of the worlds, the compassionate, the merciful, King of the day of reckoning.
Submission.	**Submission.**
(b) Thy will be done in earth as it is in heaven.	(b) Thee only do we worship and of Thee only do we ask aid.
Supplication.	**Supplication.**
(c) Give us this day our daily bread. And forgive us our debts as we forgive our debtors. And lead us not into temptation, but deliver us from evil: for Thine is the Kingdom, and the power, and the glory for ever. Amen.	(c) Guide us into the right path — the path of those to whom Thou hast been gracious, not the path of those who are the objects of wrath nor of those who have gone astray. Amen.
Matthew 6: 9–13.	The Koran

Fill in the blanks with words from the following list:

Abu al-Qasin   Ottoman Empire

Arabesque   Sacrament

Battle of Tours   Shiites

Caliphs   Sunni

Horse Archer   Umayyad

1. _____ Islamic head of state.
2. _____ Ruling Islamic family.
3. _____ The Orthodox Islamic type.
4. _____ An Islamic type.
5. _____ The battle that stopped Islamic expansion into Europe.
6. _____ Islamic soldier.
7. _____ Famous Islamic doctor.
8. _____ A type of calligraphy.
9. _____ Turkish Islamic Empire.
10. _____ Sacred reenactment of the Eucharist, of the last meal that Christ took with his disciples.

Short Answer Essay:

The coming of the Abbasid Regime had a profound influence on the Islamic world. Explain.

Fill in the blanks with words from the following list:

Armada

Basques

Bay of Biscay

Charles Martel

Iberians

Martel

Moorish Spain

Philip II

Pyrenees Mountains

Strait of Gibraltar

1. _____ Mountains separating Spain from the rest of Europe.
2. _____ The short body of water separating Africa from Spain.
3. _____ North eastern bay mostly in France.
4. _____ Spanish tribes.
5. _____ Northern Spanish tribes near the Pyrenees.
6. _____ Frankish king who defeated the Moors at Tours.
7. _____ Spanish king who launched the Armada.
8. _____ Futile Spanish attempt to conquer England in 1599.
9. _____ Islamic Spain.
10. _____ The one who stopped the Moors from conquering western Europe.

Short Answer Essay:

At the beginning of the 8th century the Moors crossed from Africa. They conquered the country swiftly except for a small bulwark in the North which would become the initial springboard for the Reconquest, which was not completed until eight centuries later (by El Cid). In 1469, the marriage of the Roman Catholic Monarchs, Isabella of Castile and Ferdinand of Aragon, marked the opening of a period of growing success for Spain, since during their reign, Granada, the last stronghold of the Moors in Spain, was conquered and, at the same time, in the same historic year of 1492, the caravels sent by the Crown of Castile under the command of Christopher Columbus discovered America. The hegemony of Spain in the Mediterranean was affirmed with the conquest of the Kingdom of Naples, and Navarre was incorporated into the Kingdom. The next two centuries, the 16th and the 17th, were the height of the Spanish Empire as a result of which the country became the world's foremost power. The defeat of the Spanish Armada initiated a long decline from which Spain never recovered. All of this probably would not have happened if the Moors had not been driven from Spain. Christopher Columbus would have never discovered the New World. The Conquistadors would have stayed home. Who do you think would have discovered the New World if Columbus had not? There is no right or wrong answer.

Fill in the blanks with words from the following list:

Barons   Peasants

Code of Chivalry   Serfs

Franks   Squires

Norsemen   Teutonic Tribes

Pages   Viking Age

1. _____ Germanic tribes.

2. _____ Barbarian tribes that lived in present-day France.

3. _____ An unwritten code of courtesy.

4. _____ Six- or seven-year-old apprentices to be knights.

5. _____ Twelve- to fourteen-year-old apprentices to be knights.

6. _____ Nobles in a feudal society.

7. _____ Poor landless serfs.

8. _____ Peasants.

9. _____ Scandinavian peoples.

10. _____ An age when Vikings conquered most of Europe.

Short Answer Essay:

Gunpowder was introduced into European warfare at the end of the Middle Ages. Predict what impact this new technology will have on warfare.

Fill in the blanks with words from the following list:

Boroughs

Bourgeois

Canterbury Tales

Cottage Industries

Divine Comedy

Epic

Monogamy

Poema del Cid

Song of Roland

Wimple

1. _____ Industries that occurred in individual homes.

2. _____ A woman's head covering.

3. _____ District of a city.

4. _____ A long narrative about a hero.

5. _____ An epic narrative about a French hero.

6. _____ An epic narrative about a Spanish hero.

7. _____ Written by Dante, the first serious literature written in Italian.

8. _____ A fictional piece written by English poet Geoffrey Chaucer.

9. _____ Inhabitants of the bourgs or burghs.

10. _____ Being faithful to one spouse.

Short Answer Essay:

The medieval experience of the exterior world took place from a perspective profoundly different from that available to people today. Both physically and conceptually, medieval people saw their world from ground level. Elevated vantage points were rare. The view from the top of the keep at Dover Castle or from the summit of the towers of Notre-Dame was as high above the ground as an individual might get, and even that experience was limited to a few people. Mountaintops provided broad panoramas, but the point of view was still land-based. While today we can see the world from above and interpret its shape on a grid of lines running north to south and east to west, medieval people saw their world from the surface, and related places to each other by landmarks, relative directions, and times of travel. What does this medieval world map tell you about the community who produced it?

Fill in the blanks with words from the following list:

Astrology

Courtly Love

Kinship and Patronage

Humors

Pottage

1. _____ Thick soup.
2. _____ Parts of the body temperament.
3. _____ Medieval code for ladies.
4. _____ What shaped society in the Middle Ages.
5. _____ Constellations and planets were thought to influence.

Short Answer Essay:

Europe's population almost doubled between 1000 and 1350; in some regions, it tripled. If life was so hard, why did the population in Europe increase so dramatically during the Middle Ages?

Fill in the blanks with words from the following list:

Carolingians

Charlemagne

Church of St. Peter

Einhard

Eusebius

Frankish Kingdom

Holy Roman Empire

Homeschooling

Pope Leo III

Primary Sources

1. _____ First Frankish monarch line.

2. _____ First medieval European empire.

3. _____ Charles the Great, ruler of the Holy Roman Empire.

4. _____ Friend of Charlemagne, who kept a diary which describes Charlemagne.

5. _____ Friend and partner with Charlemagne.

6. _____ Central European Empire.

7. _____ Early Church historian.

8. _____ The only option of education for the poor at this time.

9. _____ Firsthand references to words and ideas.

10. _____ A place cherished by Charlemagne.

Short Answer Essay:

Why do you believe so many people look back on the days of knights and ladies with such fascination?

Fill in the blanks with words from the following list:

Archbishops   Gregory the Great

Benedictine Monk   Parousia

Bishops   Scriptoria

Boniface   Theodoric

Cassiodorus   Visigoths

1. _____ First medieval pope.
2. _____ The Second Coming of Christ.
3. _____ The contemplative who founded a monastery order.
4. _____ Lower rank of Roman Catholic hierarchy.
5. _____ Higher rank of Roman Catholic hierarchy.
6. _____ Barbarian tribe.
7. _____ Apostle to the Germans.
8. _____ King of Ostrogoth people.
9. _____ Christian scholar.
10. _____ Room in a monastery devoted to copying Scripture.

Short Answer Essay:

Summarize the description of a parson (local priest), in Middle English, by English poet, Geoffrey Chaucer.

A good man was ther of religioun,
And was A POURE PERSOUN OF A TOUN;
But riche he was of hooly thoght and werk;
He was also a lerned man, a clerk,
That Cristes Gospel trewely wolde preche:
Hise parisshens devoutly wolde he teche.
Benygne he was and wonder diligent,
And in adversitee ful pacient;
And swich he was y-preved ofte sithes.
Ful looth were hym to cursen for hise tithes,
But rather wolde he geven, out of doute,
Unto his povre parisshens aboute,
Of his offryng and eek of his substaunce:
He koude in litel thyng have suffisaunce.
Wyd was his parisshe, and houses fer asonder,
But he ne lafte nat for reyn ne thonder,
In siknesse nor in meschief to visíte
The ferreste in his parisshe, muche and lite,
Upon his feet and in his hand a staf.
This noble ensample to his sheepe he gaf
That first he wroghte and afterward he taughte.
Out of the gospel he tho wordes caughte,
And this figure he added eek therto,
That if gold ruste what shal iren do?
For if a preest be foul, on whom we truste,
No wonder is a lewed man to ruste;

And shame it is, if a prest take keepe,
A shiten shepherde and a clene sheepe.
Wel oghte a preest ensample for to geve,
By his clennesse how that his sheepe sholde lyve.
He sette nat his benefice to hyre
And leet his sheep encombred in the myre,
And ran to Londoun unto Seïnt Poules
To seken hym a chaunterie for soules;
Or with a bretherhed to been withholde,
But dwelte at hoom and kepte wel his folde,
So that the wolf ne made it nat myscarie, —
He was a shepherde, and noght a mercenarie:
And though he hooly were and vertuous,
He was to synful men nat despitous,
Ne of his speche daungerous ne digne,
But in his techyng déscreet and benygne,
To drawen folk to hevene by fairnesse,
By good ensample, this was his bisynesse:
But it were any persone obstinat,
What so he were, of heigh or lough estat,
Hym wolde he snybben sharply for the nonys.
A bettre preest I trowe that nowher noon ys;
He waited after no pompe and reverence,
Ne maked him a spiced conscience,
But Cristes loore, and his Apostles twelve,
He taughte, but first he folwed it hym selve.

Fill in the blanks with words from the following list:

Cistercian Monastery

Franciscans

Julian of Norwich

Mechtild

Sixteen Revelations of Divine Love

1. _____ A Roman Catholic monastic order.
2. _____ A complex for a Roman Catholic monastic order.
3. _____ Written by Julian of Norwich.
4. _____ Wrote poetry and spiritual texts in German.
5. _____ Wrote the book *Sixteen Revelations of Divine Love*.

Short Answer Essay:

In 300 words, describe an ordinary man or woman who has been a "saint" to your life.

Fill in the blanks with words from the following list:

Italian City States

Motifs

The Holy Grail

The Teutonic Order

Saracens

1. _____ Those whom the crusaders warred against.
2. _____ Bold, sassy, and innovative entities.
3. _____ Thought to be the dish, plate, or cup used by Jesus at the Last Supper.
4. _____ Themes or ideas.
5. _____ A special group of knights from Germany.

Short Answer Essay:

Sociologist and theologian Rodney Stark's God's Battalion: Case for the Crusades argues that the Crusades were justified and necessary and were, by all means, a desirable Christian response to a real threat. It always seems counterintuitive to us today that warfare and religion can be consistent. Ideally, followers of Christ are to avoid violence and warfare. Clearly, this has not always been the case. Frequently in the crosshairs of critics are the Christian wars against Islamic people known as the Crusades, commonly viewed as the birth of European imperialism and the forced spread of Christianity. But what if we've had it all wrong? What if the Crusades were a justifiable response to a strong and determined foe? Stark argues that these bloody encounters had less to do with spreading Christianity than with responding to an ever more dangerous enemy — the emerging Islamic empire. Did Pope Leo II have it right all along?

Fill in the blanks with words from the following list:

Bartolome de las Casas

Columbus quincentenary of 1992

Ferdinand of Aragon

Isabella of Castile

October 12, 1492

1. _____ King of Spain after the Moors were driven out.
2. _____ Queen of Spain after the Moors were driven out.
3. _____ The day Columbus discovered America.
4. _____ Kept a log of Columbus' voyages.
5. _____ 500-year anniversary of Columbus' voyage.

Short Answer Essay:

Historian Felipe Fernández-Armesto traces key elements of the modern world back to the single, fateful year of 1492. "Everything changed in 1492: the way power and wealth were distributed around the globe, the way major religions and civilizations divided the world, and the increasing interconnectedness of separate economies that we now call globalization. Events that began in 1492 transformed the whole ecological system of the planet. Our individualism and the very sense we share of inhabiting one world, as partakers in a common humanity, took shape and became visible in 1492." Based upon your readings alone, agree or disagree with this statement.

Answer Key

◆ Discussion Question Answer Key

Chapter 1

Lesson 1
Answers will vary.

Lesson 2

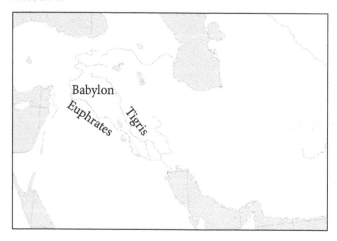

Lesson 3
Answers will vary. In my home we keep all public areas very clean and tidy. In private places, in our separate rooms, for example, tidiness is not as important an issue. Also, in my home, we never leave dirty dishes in the sink at night. It is important to my wife that we wash and put away all dishes before we go to bed.

Lesson 4
The speaker is a Jewish farmer. Farming required that farmers raise an abundant crop and save some seeds to plant next year from the harvest. The farmer in Psalm 26 has had a terrible winter; in fact, some of his family is probably ill or even dead. Nonetheless, the farmer has preserved the seed . . . "Those who sow with tears will reap with songs of joy. Those who go out weeping, carrying seed to sow, will return with songs of joy, carrying sheaves with them." The farmer believed in his God, and he believed in the harvest! Answers will vary.

Lesson 5
The gods of Sumer were immortal but human in form and demeanor. They could be hurt and no one wanted to be the one who hurt them. Each god adhered to a set of rules of divine authority known as me. They ensured that each god was able to keep the cosmos functioning according to a master plan. So it behooved Sumerians to appease the gods. Sumerians had hundreds of gods. Many had wives/husbands, children, and servants of the more powerful gods. Yes, the gods were organized into a caste system, or hierarchy, a sort of "pecking order" where the more important gods/goddesses ruled the lesser gods. The God of the Old Testament was personally involved with humankind. He created humankind in His own image. He entered a contract, or covenant, with His people. The Sumerian gods did none of these things.

Chapter 2

Lesson 1
Many, in fact, most ancient civilizations contained several competing ethnic groups who generated great diversity and energy, but, in some cases, caused friction and discord. Egypt was full of classes, but not of different ethnic groups. Even the foreign Jewish slaves were Semitic peoples. This created a fairly uneventful national development with significant, but never major, internal turmoil.

Lesson 2
Rich delta land covered the north, the Red Sea was to the West, the Arabian Desert to the East. Egypt had it all (except forests).

Lesson 3
A despot, even a bad one, offered Egypt stability. Egypt, unlike Greece, had no democratic aspirations, so this worked well for this culture. At the same time a despot, if he is insane, or unstable, can have a very negative affect too.

Lesson 4
Something like this — the Jewish people came to us in great need. We gave them food, protection, and, good honest work. And how did they thank us? They brought plagues and curses on our people. Good riddance!

Lesson 5
In the rarest of situations were Egyptian women perceived as anything but property, or, an animal. In fact, of course, some Egyptian men loved and valued their wives. But many did not. They had no theological or cultural reason to do so. In Judaism, and especially in monogamous Christianity, women were valued and treasured as the creations of God that they were. They were also valued leaders (Deborah) and influential monarchs (Esther).

Chapter 3

Lesson 1

The people of Israel trace their origin to Abraham, who established the belief that there is only one God, the creator of the universe. He did this in the midst of an alien, even hostile people. Abraham, his son Isaac and grandson Jacob all lived in the Land of Canaan, Palestine, that later came to be known as Israel.

Lesson 2

A nomadic food gatherer society is one in which most or all food is obtained from wild plants and animals, in contrast to agricultural societies which rely mainly on domesticated species.

Lesson 3

The land is rich and full of generous rivers and lakes. The Jezreel Valley, separating the hills of Galilee from those of Samaria, is Israel's richest agricultural area, cultivated by many cooperative communities called kibbutzim. Another great asset are the people who are dedicated to a glorious cause!

Lesson 4

Nomadic food gathering Israel was ruled by patriarchs in tribes and later by prophets. Then, a king was appointed. It was conquered first by Alexander the Great and then by Rome.

Lesson 5

The reader agrees with Rabbi Anteby. The Jewish people are the Chosen people and that covenant has never been fully abrogated. Answers will vary.

Chapter 4

Lesson 1

Unlike other city-states, who were managed by kings, the Indus people were ruled by groups of merchants. They had commercial links with Afghanistan, Persia, Egypt, Mesopotamia and the Samaritans.

Lesson 2

Life focused around the central fireplace called the Yagna. Dinner time was social time. The tribe would gather around the central fireplace and share news. Those who tended the central fireplace also cooked for the rest of the tribe. The clan unit was sacrosanct but meals were communal with other clans. The cooks or fire tenders were the go-between between clans, and later, mediators between the gods and the people. As the fire tenders, or cooks, prepared communal meals, Aryans would gather and share their concerns and woes. These "counseling" sessions were critical to Aryan life. It comes as no surprise, that these fire tenders later formed the caste of priests.

Lesson 3

Historians call this the "Golden Age" of ancient India. They had religious freedom. They were given free medical care, which included simple surgery. Criminals were never put to death. Instead, they were fined for their crimes. Rewards of money were given to writers, artists, and scholars to encourage them to produce wonderful work, and they did. Very few of the common people were educated, but the Gupta Empire had many universities. Students came from as far away as China to study at Gupta universities!

Lesson 4

At the top of the caste system were the Brahmin — the priests, teachers, and judges. Next came the Kshatriya, the warrior caste. The Vaisya caste were the farmers and merchants, and the Sudras were craft workers and laborers. At the bottom were the Untouchables.

Lesson 5

People were animistic and worshiped natural forces like plants and animals. Other answers may vary.

Chapter 5

Lesson 1

No one really knows. Presumably the homogeneity of Chinese culture, the strong tertiary leadership, the isolationism, and even the animist religion, contributed to Chinese ingenuity.

Lesson 2

Without consulting other sources it would be my guess that that the Chinese religions, Buddhism and Taoism, both animistic, would create static class consciousness. Also the severe feudalism that was so prevalent in ancient China generated serious class differences.

Lesson 3

The Chinese military was better trained, better organized, and, most of all, better equipped than any other far eastern army.

Lesson 4

Besides preferring a sort of isolationism, the Chinese leadership and commercial community found very little of value in Medieval Europe.

Lesson 5

By law — not custom — a Chinese woman had to obey her father and other male members in the family. On the third day of her birth, a Chinese female was place under the cot and given a piece of broken pottery to play with, and her birth was announced by giving an offering to her ancestors. Placing the baby child under the cot denoted that she is weak and she should humble herself before men. The broken pottery meant she must be laborious, while giving an offering to the ancestors denoted that one of her primary duties is to worship her elders. The young girl was not given a name; instead she was called as "daughter Number 1", "daughter Number 2" and so on. After marriage, an ancient Chinese woman would serve her husband like a slave and could not even raise her voice. Men were allowed to have more than one wife. On the other hand, if the husband of a young Chinese woman died, she was not allowed to remarry. Finally, regrettably, female infanticide was widespread.

Chapter 6

Lesson 1

Genghis Kahn was a brave, capable warrior, and a master administrator. A winning combination! A special unit supplied Mongol armies with excellent maps of the areas they were to invade, based largely on information supplied by Genghis Khan's extensive network of spies and informers. New weapons, including a variety of flaming and exploding arrows, gunpowder projectiles, and later bronze cannons, were also devised for the Mongol forces. By the time his armies rode east and west in search of plunder and conquest in the second decade of the 13th century, Genghis Khan's warriors were among the best armed and trained and the most experienced, disciplined, and mobile soldiers in the world. http://history-world.org/mongol_empire.htm

Lesson 2

While the Mongols were fearless, capable warriors, they were very mediocre administrators. They never really understood governing a sedentary, agricultural empire. They also never valued a powerful navy, something that ultimately caused them to waste a generation of young men attacking Japan.

Lesson 3

Terror tactics can conquer territory but it will never capture hearts nor sustain a long-term empire. The Mongols were forever conquering large sections of territory but losing it in a generation.

Lesson 4

The Mongols embraced a permanent nomadic lifestyle, ironically, for the simple reason that they learned to live largely on animal milk and milk products, thus tapping a new food source and, in effect, discovering a new ecological niche by displacing male lambs, calves, and colts from their mothers' teats. Lactating animals had to be tamed to allow human beings to milk them by hand, and human populations also had to adjust physiologically by continuing as adults to secrete the enzymes children need to digest their mother's milk. There was another distinct advantage to steppe life. Hundreds of domesticated animals could be managed by a few people; thus, there was a huge number of Mongol warriors left to protect from, and later to conquer, other hostile people groups. Dependence on animals meant that relatively few human beings could make a living from the vast expanse of the steppe.

Lesson 5

Khan leaders governed through a series of autonomous, tribal allies, called a confederation (union of divergent people groups united for a central purpose). At the same time, tribes and tribal confederations were always liable to break apart if the constituent groups felt aggrieved or merely distrusted the leader's luck or military skill. That was one of the reasons that the Mongols were not able to sustain a presence in conquered territories. They could subdue other people groups but could not agree how to rule them, or, more likely, the Mongols grew bored of governing a sedentary empire and sought adventure and other conquests. This was partly the motivation of Kublai Kahn when he sent his massive naval armada across the China Sea to conquer Japan. It was destroyed in a terrible storm.

Chapter 7

Lesson 1

Japan was able to maintain a distinctly "Japanese" identity while building an industrial political complex that would rival western models. While the Chinese relied on western coastal trading centers on its coast (e.g., Hong Kong), the Japanese quietly made its own industries, and the whole island became a trading center!

Lesson 2

It really took that long for Japan to build the industrial base, create a national army, and, most of all, create a competitive navy that was critical for empire building. This process was retarded somewhat by the parochial influence of local shoguns and samurai. Eventually, however, the influence of the Emperor overcame all obstacles and the Japanese burst into the international community. The historical event that made this clear was the Sino-Russian War when the Japanese annihilated the Russian fleet and army in a very quick war (1904 — 1905).

Lesson 3

The samurai, forbidden to engage in farming or business but allowed to borrow money, borrowed too much. In fact, one of the first deficit-plagued societies emerged. A growing governing class, for the first time in history, was spending more than it was producing or collecting. A rising, dangerous deficit occurred. This inevitably led to draconian taxing of the middle class, and poor, which spawned several riots. The nation had to deal somehow with samurai impoverishment and treasury deficits. The financial troubles of the samurai deteriorated their loyalties to their shogun, and the growing deficit threatened the whole system of government. One solution was reactionary — with prohibitions on spending for luxuries. Other solutions were modernizing, with the goal of increasing agrarian productivity. Whatever intervention occurred was, by any standard, unpopular and inefficient. Until Japanese society stopped spending more than it had, there was to be no prosperity. All of this led, eventually, to a powerful, tertiary, central government emerging.

Lesson 4

Literacy was highly valued but massive printing of books with machines was not. Wood block printing had been standard for centuries after 1500 Japanese printers experimented with movable type, but reverted to the wood blocks. It is one of the few examples where a civilization rejected an advance in technology to retain something it valued. The net result was that Japanese, because of supply and demand, were able, in fact had to, read a lot of western technical journals and books. In the long run this had a laudable effect on the Japanese economy. Quite literally, ironically, rejection of one technology led to the development of every other one!

Lesson 5

Japanese industry was protected in its early, vulnerable stages, because it did not have to compete with cheaper western goods. Also, the Japanese could develop its own consumer tastes and identity. At the same time it developed cheaper, often inferior goods. At first, "made in Japan" was a synonym for "poorly made."

Chapter 8

Lesson 1

Zoroastrianism shares the same beliefs as Jewish, Christian and Muslim beliefs concerning God and Satan, eternal judgment, Heaven and hell, the Virgin Birth, slaughter of the innocents, Resurrection, and the Final Judgment. In Zoroastrianism, the Creator Ahura Mazda is all good, and no evil originates from him. Thus, in Zoroastrianism good and evil have distinct sources, with evil trying to destroy God. So, Zoroastrianism is a dualistic religion, with a clear concept of good and evil. Mazda, though, is not omniscient, or omnipotent, like the Judeo-Christian God, but he is all, completely, good. Our God is both good and in complete control of the universe. In our faith, God is not dueling with Satan — no — God is the Lord of Heaven and Hell. All He has to do is think that Satan is destroyed and he is destroyed! Mazda, however, is fighting, even now with Satan. Zoroastrianism has sacred Scriptures. Their most important texts are those of the Avesta, of which a significant portion has been lost, and mostly only the liturgies (orders of worship) have survived. Zoroastrianism Scripture is inspiring, but not inspired! It is not the inerrant, infallible Word of God like our Bible! Zoroastrianism followers worship in temples with priests. But the priests do not perform any expiation (sacrifice) for sins. This is curious since Zoroastrianism espouses a moral system. Followers must not marry outside the faith, for instance. Homosexuality is a sinful lifestyle. But Zoroastrianism offers no satisfactory way for redemption. Finally, there is no conversion. Followers are either born into the faith, or they experience an unsolicited revelation. But adherents are forbidden to share their faith with others. By the time Christ came to live among us, Zoroastrianism was more or less an ancient religion. But during its day it was one of the most powerful and influential religions on the Middle East. www.zoroastrianism.com/

Lesson 2

Confucius believed that human beings could acquire a sort of utopia through adherence to a series of wise sayings or aphorisms. Many, including this author, feel that Confucius felt no so such thing. The notion that his writings would be a religion or even a world view philosophy would have been laughable to Confucius.

Lesson 3

Redemption is a historical, actual fact accomplished by a man, Jesus Christ, the Son of the Living God. It was not a metaphor, not a revelation. It was a fact.

Lesson 4

Taoism refers to a philosophical or religious tradition in which the basic concept is to establish harmony with the Tao, which is the origin of everything that exists. The word "Tao" means "nature" as in the nature of all things as well as the natural world. Christianity, invites mankind into a relationship with the Deity through relationship with His Son. Taoist propriety and ethics emphasize the Three Jewels of the Tao: compassion, moderation, and humility. Taoist thought generally focuses on nature, the relationship between humanity and the cosmos; health and longevity; and wu wei (action through inaction). Christian ethics are based on the inerrant, inspired Word of God. Reverence for ancestor spirits is common in Taoism. While there is no savior or ubiquitous metaphysical god, there are eight immortals — and more. Laozi — the founder of Taoism. But countless are the numbers of hermits and wandering Taoist sages, whose levels of realization were known only to themselves — and perhaps also their equally anonymous teachers! Christianity is based on a personal relationship with a very much alive Savior. Revelation, while still occurring, must concur with the Word of God (the Bible).

Lesson 5

Hinduism invites its adherents to a higher consciousness, a sort of peace, but not one single god, among millions, died for humankind.

Chapter 9

Lesson 1

The Minoans were a very sophisticated culture and had opened trade with the Phoenicians and other people groups in the region. This led to an exchange of culture and ideas which became not only established as part of Minoan culture but spread to influence cultures, religion and government all over the Aegean islands and mainland Greece. Thus, from the beginning, Greek culture was freely interacting with neighboring cultures and both influenced and was influenced, by other cultures. In fact, Minoa was the first people group to develop a merchant marine fleet that facilitated trade all over the known world.

Lesson 2

The physical features of the country exercised an important influence upon the political destinies of the people. Greece is one of the most mountainous countries of Europe. Its surface is occupied by a number of small plains, either entirely surrounded by limestone mountains or open only to the sea. Each of the principal Grecian cities was founded in one of these small plains; and, as the mountains which separated it from its neighbors were lofty and rugged, each city grew up in solitary independence. But at the same time it had ready and easy access to the sea, and Arcadia was almost the only political division that did not possess some territory upon the coast. Thus shut out from their neighbors by mountains, the Greeks were naturally attracted to the sea, and became a maritime people. Hence they possessed the love of freedom and the spirit of adventure, which have always characterized, more or less the inhabitants of maritime districts. –William Smith, *The Smaller History of Greece.*

Lesson 3

Answers will vary.

Lesson 4

The late 19th century successful stand of a few hundred British soldiers against thousands of Zulu warriors in the Zulu Wars. Israeli victory against the Arab states in the 1967 War.

Lesson 5

Democracy has never been, and will never be, a popular form of government. Most leadership groups find the notion of rule by the people to be far too threatening. In some cases democracy has not worked very well. Historians Loren Haarsma and Andrew Mark Kuchling wrote, "Perhaps the biggest problem with Democracy is that people tend to get exactly the government that they deserve. For example, in many modern-day democracies, the people claim that they want their government to operate under a balanced budget, when in fact this is the farthest thing from the truth. What the people really want, as they repeatedly demonstrate from their voting, is decreased taxes and increased government spending — particularly when it comes to government projects which directly benefit themselves. Professional politicians, if by nothing else than by a simple Darwinian processes, are very good at perceiving such things, and give the people exactly want: huge government deficits. For example, in every present and past democracy, the people always claim that they want politicians who will not accept bribes, when in fact this is the farthest thing from the truth. What the people really want, as they repeatedly demonstrate from the voting, is politicians who will spend huge amounts of money on multi-media campaigns to win votes, who will spend massive amounts of time coming to their towns to speak to the local rotary club or school (for a fee), and who will spend massive amounts of time influencing legislation to win government contracts for local businesses." http://www.galactic-guide.com/articles/2S3.html

Chapter 10

Lesson 1

The Roman Empire emphasized the state and state power over the individual. The medieval Roman Catholic Church emphasized humankind in relationship and a reflection of God. During the Renaissance mankind again was the primary subject of interest to artists and to philosophers.

Lesson 2

Tragedies were part of a religious festival to Dionysus. On each of three days, three tragedies and a satyr-play were presented by the same poet. "Tragedy is an achievement that is peculiarly Greek," scholar Edith Hamilton writes. "It concerns the entire people . . . who felt the appeal of the tragic to such a degree that they would gather thirty thousand strong to see a performance." Greek drama, like a religious liturgy, celebrates and explores human life.

Lesson 3

The theatre of the later fifth century BC consisted of a large circular orchestra for the chorus, surrounded by the audience; on the other side was a low stage offering easy communication with the orchestra. There was of course no sound equipment so this was very necessary. Behind the stage was some kind of building where actors could hide. The chorus could enter the orchestra from either side. The chorus (from 12 to 15 people) sang and danced; their leader might engage informally in dialogue with the actors — there were no actresses. Greek tragedies and comedies were always performed in outdoor theaters and occurred in the daytime. American theater normally occurs indoors, in a well-lighted facility, and almost never includes a chorus.

Lesson 4

"On these two scores it is easy to explain what at first sight seems puzzling, his great unpopularity in his lifetime and his unexampled popularity shortly after his death. Only five of his plays were awarded a first prize, whereas Sophocles gained over twenty. Aristophanes has good words for Aeschylus and higher praise for Sophocles but nothing is too bad for him to say about Euripides. The modern mind is never popular in its own day. People hate being made to think, above all upon fundamental problems. Sophocles touched with the radiant glory of sublime poetry the figures of the ancient gods, and the Athenians went home from his plays with the pleasing conviction that old things were right. But Euripides was the arch-heretic, miserably disturbing, never willing to leave a man comfortably ensconced in his favorite convictions and prejudices. Prizes were not for such as he. And yet, very soon after his death, the verdict swung far to the other side and extraordinary tales of the way he was loved by all manner of men have come down to us." — Edith Hamilton.

Lesson 5

The Archaic period was the earliest period in Greek sculpture, which started around 600 B.C. and lasted until 480 BC. These works have a stiff and ridged appearance similar to that of the Egyptian sculpture. The second period, the Classical period, was between the Archaic and Hellenistic times. The Classical period exhibits a more realistic and sometimes idealistic portrayal of the human figure. Many sculpture figures had robes. The robes gave the sculpture the idea of movement and realism in an effort by the artist to show humans more realistically. The third period, the Hellenistic period, started a little before 300 BC. These works idealized the individual and in a way, attempted to capture the idea of youth and strength in their design. The works no longer emphasized the nude human body — Greek sculpture wanted to go much farther into the human soul and psyche.

Chapter 11

Lesson 1

Alexander was raised in the court of a king and educated by the great Aristotle. Perhaps this influence, along with the influence of his very capable, warrior king, father, presaged the great conqueror that Alexander would become. As one biographer explains, "The secret of Alexander's success was his character. He possessed a certain combination of mental and personal attractions, which in every age gives to those who exhibit it a mysterious and almost unbounded ascendency over all within their influence. Alexander was characterized by these qualities in a very remarkable degree. He was finely formed in person, and very prepossessing in his manners. He was active, athletic, and full of ardor and enthusiasm in all that he did. At the same time, he was calm, collected, and considerate in emergencies requiring caution, and thoughtful and far-seeing in respect to the bearings and consequences of his acts. He formed strong attachments, was grateful for kindnesses shown to him, considerate in respect to the feelings of all who were connected with him in any way, faithful to his friends, and generous toward his foes. In a word, he had a noble character, though he devoted its energies unfortunately to conquest and war. He lived, in fact, in an age when great personal and mental powers had scarcely any other field for their exercise than this. He entered upon his career with great ardor, and the position in which he was placed gave him the opportunity to act in it with prodigious effect."

Lesson 2

For the first time the soldier Alexander now had to become the administrator Alexander — of an expanding empire. He chose to establish outposts of Greek culture. Believing in the superiority of Greek culture, instead of building jails and military outposts, he built huge libraries to house Greek books and culture. In Egypt, for instance, he founded the greatest of the cities known by his name — Alexandria. Alexander did not merely want to conquer armies; he wanted to win the hearts of men and women to Greek culture and ideas.

Lesson 3

Hellenism is a term generally used by historians to refer to the period from the death of Alexander the Great (323 BC) to the death of Cleopatra and the incorporation of Egypt in the Roman Empire in 30 BC. Egypt was the last important survivor of the political system which had developed as a consequence both of the victories of Alexander and of his premature death. The word Hellenism is also used to indicate more generically the cultural tradition of the Greek-speaking part of the Roman Empire between Augustus and Justinian and/or the influence of Greek civilization on Rome, Carthage, India, and other regions which were never part of the empire of Alexander. Finally, Hellenization is used with reference to Judea, Persia, to indicate the penetration of elements of Greek civilization into territories which, though subject to Greco-Macedonian rule for a certain period of time, preserved their national culture with conspicuous success (e.g., Israel). The early Church was founded in a Hellenistic world and this no doubt affected the way it emerged. Thanks to Rome, there was stability in the entire Empire. Although there was persecution, Christians could travel with ease across the known world to share the Gospel. Thanks to Hellenism, most of the known world was educated and ready to read the Letters of Paul, or to understand the philosophical intricacies of the Gospel. http://www.jewishvirtuallibrary.org/

Lesson 4

Alexander was a ruthless, cruel, unforgiving conqueror and a poor administrator/emperor. "Thus, we can see how the historical Alexander has faded into the invincible general, the great leader, explorer and king, as time continued, especially in the Middle Ages with its world of chivalry, warriors and great battles: a superb context into which to fit Alexander, even if this meant distortion of the truth, and history subsumed to legend. Indeed, during the Middle Ages [he] was regarded as one of the four great kings of the ancient world." The author agrees with Worthington. Alexander exhibited very little character and did almost nothing to advance any agenda but his own.

Lesson 5

Answers will vary but might include:
1. The Bible
2. *The Republic*, Plato,
3. *Odyssey*, Homer
4. *War and Peace*, Leo Tolstoy
5. *Paradise Lost*, John Milton
6. *Sound and Fury*, William Faulkner
7. *The Rivals*, Richard Sheridan
8. *Murder in the Cathedral*, T. S. Eliot
9. *Heart of Darkness*, Joseph Conrad
10. Plays, William Shakespeare

Chapter 12

Lesson 1

I would predict that the Etruscans and the Greeks will not be friends! Rome had many advantages right from the start. Like many Greek city states, for example Athens, Rome lies only a few miles from the sea. It was close enough to trade with Mediterranean markets but far enough to be safe from Phoenicians and other seafaring raiders. But it was different from Athens in other, important ways. For one thing, Rome lay in a vast, and rich plain that promised agricultural support for the bustling city that grew at a phenomenal rate. Also, Rome lies central to the Italian peninsula, which in turn lies central to the entire Mediterranean Sea. Italy is guarded by the Alps to the North and by the sea all around. Speaking of the Greeks, they did help the early Romans a lot. The Greeks, who had no desire to control the geo political world in Italy, brought commerce, technology, and stability to Southern Italy. From the Greeks the Romans learned fundamental skills such as reading and writing, even their religion is almost entirely derived from Greek mythology. If the Greeks, who were no threat, settled to the south of them, then the Roman had the Etruscans to the north. It was a great threat. Etruria, too, was predominantly an urban society, drawing its considerable wealth from seaborne trade. The wealthy Etruscans were generally seen by ancient Romans and Greeks to be decadent and weak. So there was no love loss between the Etruscans and the Greeks.

Lesson 2

It felt threatened from enemies without and within. Also, Rome became so big many Roman officials it must be ruled by one leader.

Lesson 3

This is true. A nation that claims to be completely tolerant can be dogmatic in its toleration! The Romans, for instance, told the Jewish people, you will accept our gods, like we accept yours, or we will kill you! Since Roman religion was not founded on some core belief that ruled out other religions, foreign religions found it relatively easy to establish themselves in the imperial capital itself. For that reason, among others, Christianity, when it came, spread like wildfire across the Roman Empire. In summary, Rome was the first secular state that presaged the modern states that would follow. While it gave lip service to religion and its enculturation advantages, in fact, Rome was very chivalric about its religions. Its world view was clearly motivated by secular, concrete, earthly concerns more than metaphysical reality and, when religions like Christianity, with its claim that Jesus was the only way, the only truth, and the only life, came knocking at the Roman religious door, it found itself unwelcome.

Lesson 4

Roman young people were perceived as young adults. "Play" was not encouraged. Nobody "fell in love" or chose his/her own spouse. It was the Roman custom to arranging marriages for boys and girls when they were still very young. They would then need to wait until she became an adult (15 or 16) until the marriage could take place. Being betrothed for such a lengthy time generally meant for girls to lead a very sheltered life. To flirt, or even simply being in contact with other boys or could be seen as an abrogation of the marriage arrangements.

Lesson 5

Roman farmers were the best in the world. They produced huge surpluses that assured the health and wealth of Rome. The empire was built on their backs. The production and transportation of foods dominated the trading industry, and encouraged a vast exchange of other goods from all parts of Europe, Asia, and Africa. The prosperity of the empire and many of it citizens generated a need for luxurious imports. Silks from China, cotton from Egypt, and spices from India, Ivory and wild animals from Africa, iron ore from Spain and Britain, valuable gems from Germany and slaves from all over the enriched the Roman economy. However, industry and manufacturing was always in the shadow of agriculture. Agriculture was the big mega-industry of Rome.

Chapter 13

Lesson 1

Christians made a bold assertion: Jesus Christ was the promised Messiah, the Son of the Living God. This was something completely new in the metaphysical world that existed in the first century. Christians loved one another; they met in homes and welcomed everyone into the fellowship, male, female, slave, and free. In Antioch they quite literally crossed over walls created to keep races and ethnic groups separated. Africans, former Jews, converted gentiles all worshipped and fellowshipped together in this most inclusive of early religions. There was absolutely no religion quite like it and it literally conquered the known world in one generation.

Lesson 2

It was not easy to be a young person in a first century Christian or Jewish household. Everyone had two meals a day — no one, except the Romans, would eat lunch. The main staple was unleavened, or flat bread, much like Mexican chaparejos. Breakfast consisted of bread, olives, dates, and dry cheese. Dinners were about the same but with some fish or lamb thrown in. The vast majority of Palestinians lived in cities. Jesus lived close to three major ancient cities. The ancient capital of Galilee, Sepphoris, and Nazareth. Cities were no more than 500 to perhaps a thousand people. They were dark and unsavory places to many — sewage was flowing in the streets and there was no effort to control wood fires and smoke. Young people would have seen their rabbi read from papyrus rolls, which were often more than 30 feet long! Or they would attend Christian home meetings.

Lesson 3

The first part of an early Christian worship assembly, held at first in homes, was open to all, including strangers, who might be converted by the fellowship and preaching. Every church service had a meal during this time, and, at the end, in a very informal way, communion, the Lord's Supper, was served. This part of the service involved the Lord's Supper, which only the baptized were allowed to partake, so the seekers departed then. While there was no official altar call, nor was there a calling forth of the "gifts," it was during this time that miracles — healings in particular — occurred. These were very natural phenomenon without any deliberate, emotional conjuring by the leadership. Prophecy and other gifts were encouraged and common.

There was no Bible of course. Paul's epistles were available by the middle of the first century, and, then, slowly, Matthew, Mark, Luke, and then John wrote their Gospels. Of course, again, though, copies were few and far between. So, mostly, teaching was based on these early works, and a non-canonical work, the Didache. The Bible would come later. Repentance was an involved process in the early church. Privatism (the notion that the individual alone is important in society) is a modern phenomenon. Sin was not a personal matter but as something that destroyed the unity of the church. Penitents fasted and prayed for the forgiveness of their sins, appeared before the church to make public confession, and were barred from the Lord's Supper until they gave evidence of a change of heart and were absolved. The Lord's Supper, or Agape meal, was reserved for the last event in the afternoon or early evening service.

Lesson 4

Answers will vary but might include the following. Of course all believers live in relationship with their Lord and one another in fellowship. The Lord's Supper is practiced, but except in the Roman Catholic Church, not in any frequency as it was in the early church. While there are some Christians who are persecuted, it is not in the same number and degree that occurred in the early decades after Christ walked the Earth.

Lesson 5

It is critical that Christians do not overcome evil with evil but that they overcome evil with good (Rom. 12:21).

Chapter 14

Lesson 1

Never in the history of the world has a religion so honored and empowered women as completely as Christianity. Women were the last disciples at the cross and the first at the empty tomb. They remained a central part of the Christian Church. Women shared the pastoral role with their husbands; women manifested many early spiritual gifts. Women were esteemed and honored by all in the Christian Church. Christianity was the first religion to do so. Women were not merely "honored and esteemed." They were an important reason that the Church grew so quickly. They were valued church members. In fact the church was the only community entity that really valued women.

Early church leaders acknowledged that there were more women than in other faiths but this was a distinct advantage. It wasn't that Christian leaders were in favor of "women's liberation." The fact was that women were a critical part of the infrastructure that emerged in the first century. They cooked and served the meals during home church meetings. They freely manifested supernatural gifts in church services. They were prayer warriors. They were tireless workers on behalf of our Lord! Women were hard workers and, ironically, as a labor force, were readily available. As society enjoyed the enforced peace and security of Roman occupation, women had more and more spare time. They used it to advance the cause of Christ.

Lesson 2

The early Church could focus on people and their needs with virtually no distractions concerning institutional demands. For more than 150 years after the Resurrection, some argue it was longer — up to 300 years, Christians had no official church buildings. During this time, evangelism was conducted mainly in homes, in the context of worship and care giving. There were virtually no evangelists or revival services. Friends were invited to the potluck dinners that were the heart of early church liturgies. Towards the end of the service, unsaved visitors were invited to commit their hearts to Christ, and, if they agreed, they were invited to the last, most important ritual, the agape meal (the Lord's Supper). Then, in the next few weeks the new converts "crossed the Jordan" or were baptized in the Jordan River. It is unlikely that the first converts were immersed. Nor were they "sprinkled." It is likely that early converts had water poured over their heads as they stood in the shallow Jordan River. They were now members of the Body of Christ, the Church! It was generally expected that everyone would participate in a religion of some sort, but few people thought it necessary to take religion seriously. When a people group — like the Christians — really took their religion seriously, it makes a great impact on first century society.

Lesson 3

Gnosticism drew many converts away from the Gospel. Gnosticism argued that Jesus was not really a man. Not all defenders of orthodoxy stayed orthodox themselves. Tertullian and Novatian, for example, two major anti-Gnostic theologians of the 200s, each fell out of favor with the church: Tertullian, because of his conversion to the Montanist heresy; Novatian, because of his unforgiving stance against those who had denied Christ under persecution. Heretics often provided a great service to the church. For example, Marcion rejected the Old Testament and the Gospels of Matthew, Mark, and John, thus forcing the church to define the New Testament canon. It is fair to say we would not have had a Bible without Marcion. Arius, in denying the deity of Christ, made the church articulate the Nicene Creed that became critical to early Christian orthodoxy.

Lesson 4

Until the middle of the second century there was no Bible. In fact, most people did not see much of a need. For one thing, the early church had Paul's letters that were circulating through the churches. At the same time, there were no church buildings and therefore no church property and no church infrastructure to maintain. Besides there was no need for a systematic church dogma because there was no aberrant serious alternative church dogma. That was to change.

Lesson 5

As the Church matured, a group of radical Christians emerged. These people were called the Desert Fathers. The Desert Fathers were hermits and ascetics who lived mainly in the Egyptian desert beginning around the third century AD. The most famous was Anthony the Great, who moved into the desert in 270–271. He founded desert monasticism. Monasticism was a relatively new idea in Christianity. A Monastic, or monk, purposed to live a sheltered life so as to concentrate on God alone. Some monks lived solitary lives, taking a vow of silence. Others lived openly in community.

Chapter 15

Lesson 1

Always the darling intellectual, and wishing to advance himself politically, the ambitious Augustine thrived in the politically correct Manichean sect. Augustine, who could not escape the prayers and silent moral turpitude of his faithful mother, found the Manicheans a most desirable escape from what Augustine saw as the demanding Christian faith. Manichean faith claimed that security could be attained without sacrifice, and guilt removed without atonement. The world the Manicheans imagined was dualistic, competing

between two contrary powers: the perfectly good creator and the perfectly evil destroyer. The convert could obtain salvation by intellectually overcoming the Devil, who, after all, was not that clever. If the devil did cause one to sin, then he need not feel guilt because, the Manichean, after all, was saved through knowledge, not through any religious act. What a metaphysical deal! If it was only true!

Lesson 2

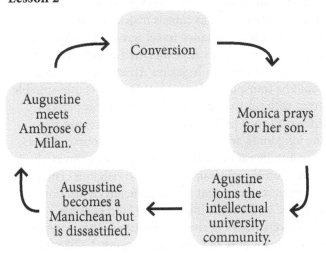

Lesson 3

Strong executive leadership would make the most of leadership in a church that was growing exponentially. At the same time, a strong episcopacy could control aberrant theology and heresy. At the same time, some of the personal, human touch of ministry would be replaced by administrative protocol. At times, the spontaneity of the Holy Spirit was defined as disunity.

Lesson 4

While one is sympathetic with the Donatists, to isolate weak believers and proclaim that they cannot ever be redeemed and forgiven, except in the most strenuous conditions, is to invite disaster in the Church.

Lesson 5

In the time of Augustine, and today, Christians are called to excellence and to courage. "Look around at all that God has done, and give thanks. And then go forth, Elijahs, and challenge the gods of this age — at Harvard, at the Supreme Court, in Hollywood. Give no quarter and ask for none. We must give God everything we are and will ever be. The God we serve deserves nothing less, accepts nothing less!"

Chapter 16

Lesson 1

In many ways, African kingdoms, isolated on a continent, developed in unique and significant ways. Besides Egypt, there were two distinct kingdoms: Ghana and Mali. The Sahel, which is the region of West Africa just south of the Sahara Desert, a vast and inhospitable place, became established as an important area of trade around A.D. 700. Advancements in transportation, such as camels instead of horses, allowed for long-distance travel across the Sahara. This one event, more than any other, had a profound impact on the economy of Sub-Sahara Africa. Commodities could be transported long distances across inhospitable areas with relative ease. Trade with various parts of Africa, Europe and Asia connected this region and the kingdoms, which arose in it. In the course of less than a millennium, it flourished at varying times as an economic, political, cultural and religious center. It is extraordinary that such significant civilizations emerged in the most inhospitable land possible. These were not rich, river civilizations. They emerged primarily because of their trading savvy. Unlike the Mongols, who conquered through military hegemony, these African kingdoms emerged through commercial hegemony. Thus these kingdoms never developed a military class and army and were vulnerable when Islamic and western invasions occurred in the early 17th century. In summary, African kingdoms originally arose on the edge of inhospitable deserts, not in river valleys, but they prospered because of their commercial savvy.

Lesson 2

After A.D. 500, Ghana emerged as a thriving nation, becoming an established center of the iron industry. Skilled ironworkers produced weapons which made Ghana the leading military, industrial state of the continent. Ghana had the equivalent of the American defense industrial base! No other nation or people group could produce the quality weapons that Ghana did. Thus, with its technological weapons, Ghana maintained a mobile, aggressive, and highly effective military force that ruled one-half of the African continent. The riches of Ghana would have rivaled the most extravagant Chinese emperor or Egyptian pharaoh. From approximately A.D. 300 through the mid-1000s, Ghana rivaled Rome as the most thriving trading center in the world. Arab caravans traveled on camels from North Africa across the Sahara to exchange salt, dried fruits, and copper for Ghanaian gold, ivory, leather goods, and jewelry. Artisans crafted gold and exotic wooden products. At the same time, Ghana developed a vital agrarian industry. Much like the present American economy, Ghanaian agriculture was a minor part of the larger economy. But its farmers harvested cocoa, plantains, yams, corn, and peanuts in abundant levels. Ghana, then, while remaining primarily a nomadic nation, was able to maintain a flourishing agrarian economy that fed the entire Empire and even provided products as far away as Egypt. Fishing and forestry were also thriving industries.

Lesson 3

Ghana, and subsequent African kingdoms, prospered because of their economic success; not because of military victories. Admittedly much warfare goes on among nations, enabling the ruler of the most powerful state to demand the submission of the others. But this is only the background to the main business of controlling the caravans of merchants and camels. Ghana was well placed to control the traffic in gold from the valley of the Senegal River. While gold was the most valuable African commodity, unfortunately slavery was a close second. Ghana also exported other exotic and very valuable products. These included elephant tusks, ostrich feathers and the cola nut popular in precursors of the carbonated soft drink. After the gold and slavery trade, the most important commodity coming south with the caravans was salt, essential in the diet of African agricultural communities. The salt mines of the Sahara were extremely valuable. Salt was a valuable seasoning and preserving agent and there was great demand for it. There is evidence that even European and Asian traders bought Ghanaian salt. In summary, because Ghana was able to sustain a successful, and highly profitable culture in the midst of such an inhospitable environment is a remarkable testimony to this ingenious people group who, in their time, was one of the most advanced, civilized people group in the world.

Lesson 4

In its day, the Mali Empire was huge. Its mercantile approach was not unlike the earlier Athenian Empire and colonies. The Mali Empire was based on outlying areas — even small kingdoms — pledging allegiance to Mali and giving annual tribute in the form of rice, millet, lances, and arrows. Slaves were used to clear new farmlands where beans, rice, sorghum, millet, papaya, gourds, cotton, and peanuts were planted. Cattle, sheep, goats, and poultry were bred. Agriculture, quite literarily, became "gold" to Mali. As the population in Africa increased astronomically, the Mali officials were ready to provide food and sustenance and they had a trading industry to make it possible.

Like Ghana, Mali prospered from the taxes it collected on trade in the empire. All goods passing in, out of, and through the empire were heavily taxed. Mali was so rich that it did not barter a great deal. Gold was used as currency.

Lesson 5

Most historians concluded that European Caucasian cultures never took African cultures very seriously. The notion that Timbuktu would be as sophisticated and wealthy as Paris, for instance, was unthinkable. Inferior people groups just could not do that.

Chapter 17

Lesson 1

Whatever they ate, wherever they lived, Native Americans were mostly nomads. They would build cities, large cities, but, these cities were abandoned as the seasons of the year changed. During and after this period two regions of North America develop quite advanced agrarian societies — the Mississippi valley and the southwest. Farming, accompanied by village life, spreads up the east coast, where fields were cleared from the woodlands for the planting of maize. But in most parts of the continent the tribes continue to live a semi-nomadic existence, in the traditional manner of hunter-gatherers, even though they lack the one animal which makes movement on the plains easy.

A peculiar Native American habit was mound building. From about 1000 BC great burial mounds were constructed around tomb chambers of log or wood. The earliest burial mounds in north America were those of the Adena culture of the Ohio valley, closely followed by nearby Hopewell tribes. The period of greatest activity is from the first century BC to the AD fifth century, by which time a vast number of mounds were built throughout North America.

Lesson 2

No one really knows; however, there are several theories. One theory states that a severe drought, of long duration, caused these agricultural centers to disappear. Native Americans were forced to return to a nomadic existence. Another theory states that there were earthquakes. There is an earthquake fault in the Mississippi Valley. Another theory suggests that a serious of wars erupted in the central North American area and Native peoples destroyed several cities. The most likely explanation, though, is that many of the Mississippian peoples, and other city builders, merely

decided to return to a nomadic life. Because of weather changes, or other advantages, city dwelling Native Americans may have simply returned to their nomadic ways. This is the case with the Dakota Sioux and the Cheyenne. Why couldn't the city builders do the same?

Lesson 3

Answers will vary. This author would prefer the Cheyenne who lived on the open plains and practice monogamous marriages.

Lesson 4

Kinship ties — based on bloodlines and marriage — were very important to Native Americans. Kinship formed the basis of the political, economic, and religious system. In other words, in Native American culture, kinship was the primary sociological function in Native American society. Native American kinship systems were pervasive and intricate. They included regulations governing marriages, relations with in-laws, and even domicile after marriage. Most Native American groups placed less emphasis on the nuclear family and more upon the tribe. One sign of the relative unimportance of the nuclear family as opposed to larger kinship ties is that many Native American societies provided for relatively easy access to divorce.

Lesson 5

The Plains Native Americans by the 16th century were totally dependent upon the horse. The horse enabled the Plains Native Americans to gain their food with relative ease from the seemingly limitless buffalo herds. The horse enabled villages to spend more time in culture building activities like artisan crafts and religious rituals. The horse enabled the Plains Native Americans to travel faster and further in search of bison herds and to transport more goods, thus enjoying a richer material environment than their pedestrian ancestors. The horse impacted Native American culture than the railroad changed early western culture.

Chapter 18

Lesson 1

The continent's topography is often likened to a huge football stadium owing to its flat interior almost ringed by high mountains. There are three main topographic features: the Andes, central rain forests, and the extensive Brazilian high country.

In their northern parts the Andes exhibit expansive plateau and valleys. These contain three of the world's highest capitals: Bogotá, Quito and highest of all, La Paz, Bolivia. The Andes also exhibit several glaciers. The climate of South America is a study of extremes. The arid Andes meet the torrid, humid Amazon jungles in east Peru.

The very fertile soils from the erosion of the Andes formed the basis for early Native American people groups. Nearly all settled, and expanded from these areas. Only in Greece did geography have such a profound impact on people groups as that which exists in South America.

Lesson 2

Far from the rest of the world, far from western culture, religion, and commercial practices, Central and South American, and for that matter, North American people groups experienced relatively uninterrupted prosperity for more than one thousand years. More importantly, as time will tell, isolationism protected Native people from horrible diseases that would later kill more Native people than any other single catastrophe.

Lesson 3

While Christianity is comfortable with the supernatural, the Bible states that men and animals alone are alive. And mankind alone is created in the image of God!

Lesson 4

The most popular theory for the decline of the Mayans was climate change. There was precedence. Around the year 800, the Yucatan suffered a 200-year drought and it left the region drier than it had ever been. This makes sense. The Mayas survival relied on the cultivation of their crops, such as Maize, which requires rainfall. With this 200-year long drought, the soil would have gone almost completely dry and there would be crop failure resulting in widespread famine and probably susceptibility to disease as well.

Lesson 5

The Incas were the last people group to be conquered by the Spanish. They remained relatively safe, and isolated, throughout their short era. The topography of the Andes and frequent earthquakes encouraged the Incas to build huge, solid structures and cities. The people developed strong family ties and were fierce warriors.

Chapter 19

Lesson 1

This is absolutely untrue and shows Edward Gibbon's pro-western prejudices! The Byzantine Empire was a vigorous presence in the eastern Roman Empire for a thousand years after Rome fell. It made great contributions to civilization: Hellenism with all its rich heritage was preserved for posterity. The Roman Empire, the best of it at least (i. e., legal system) was preserved. The Greek Orthodox church brought thousands of Turks (Armenians), Russians, and Slavic people to Christ.

Situated at the crossroads of east and west, Constantinople acted as the disseminator of culture for all peoples who came in contact with the empire. By the time the empire collapsed in 1453, the western and eastern world had indelibly been marked by the splendor that was Byzantium!

Lesson 2

Justinian revived the Roman Empire and recovered the lost western half of the Empire. Although his achievements were short term, he accomplished a lot. He also established a law code that was based on legal precedence — a major breakthrough in the rule of law. Its affect on western law is comparable to the Magna Carta. His reign also marked a revival of Byzantine culture, particularly in church buildings, which made Constantinople the center of Eastern Orthodox Christianity for many centuries. Justinian was able to enervate the two most important institutions in Byzantium: the army and the Church.

Lesson 3

The Bosporus Strait is considered the boundary between Europe and Asia. It has always been strategically important, and control over it has been an objective of a number of hostilities in modern history. Certainly this was the case during the Byzantium period.

Lesson 4

AD 1054 designates the very first major division in Christianity and the beginning of "denominations." Disagreement between these two branches of Christendom had already long existed, but the widening gap between the Roman and Eastern churches increased until there were two different Christian churches. On religious matters the two branches disagreed over issues pertaining to the nature of the Holy Spirit, the use of icons in worship and the correct date for celebrating Easter. Cultural differences played a major role too, with the Eastern mindset more inclined toward philosophy, mysticism, and ideology, and the Western outlook guided more by a practical and legal mentality.

Lesson 5

The Black Death, or the Bubonic Plague, the most severe epidemic in human history, ravaged Europe, in the sixth century, and from 1347–1351. Twenty-five million people (one third of Europe's population at the time) were killed during this short period. Life was in total chaos. The plague was a disaster without parallel, causing dramatic changes in Europe and Asia. The Black Death had many effects beyond its immediate symptoms. Not only did the Black Death take a devastating toll on human life, but it also played a major role in shaping European life in the years that followed. Whole areas were depopulated and for the first time the survivors experienced a surplus of food. The plague discouraged urbanization for a thousand years, and, during this period, the world again became a predominantly rural area.

Chapter 20

Lesson 1

The Kievan Russians became the preeminent power in Russia by drawing on the strength of the Byzantium Empire. Kievan Russians were very impressed with Byzantium and ties were very strong. They introduced a Slavic variant of the Eastern Orthodox religion, making a synthesis of Byzantine and Slavic cultures that defined Russian culture for the next thousand years. Thus, the Church, more than any other institution, created the Russian character.

Lesson 2

Russia benefited from the Tatar invasions. Besides the revelation of having a strong central government, the Russians overcame significant ethnic differences to defeat the cruel, ruthless Tatars. After the Tatars departed, familial ties remained that ultimately led to the genesis of the Russian nation. At the same time, power shifted from the southern, more vulnerable capital of Kiev, to the more northern capital of Moscow. Founded in the 12th century, the Principality of Muscovy, was able to emerge from more than 200 years of Mongol domination (13th–15th centuries) and to gradually conquer and absorb surrounding principalities. In the early 17th century, a new Romanov Dynasty continued this policy of expansion across Siberia to the Pacific. So the Tatars united ethnic rich Russia and moved the capital to the more western European Moscow.

Lesson 3

Russia includes almost unlimited natural resources, but can you imagine governing and unifying such a huge country?

Lesson 4

Every historical event is perceived through the prism of Christianity.

Lesson 5

A new trading center grew at Moscow. Between 1237 and 1240 Kievan Rus was finally crushed by the onslaught of the Tatars The once-flourishing populace either perished or fled into the neighboring forests. After the Tatar invasions, the Russian epicenter moved to the Northwest to Moscow.

Chapter 21

Lesson 1

Poor Eastern Europe is at the crossroads of Europe. At the end of the first Millennium of the New Era, all of central and Eastern Europe was beginning to stabilize. For the next thousand years, continued pressure existed. From the west the Germans pushed relentlessly eastward. From the east, for several centuries transient onslaughts of Mongols and Tatars caused devastation, and later the growing Russian empire pushed westward. From the south the Turks pushed northward. The net result is that even today, the Balkans are a volatile area.

Lesson 2

The Germanic people were intensely loyal to their kin, but, violent and choleric toward outsiders. Germanic government was somewhat democratic since the chieftain ruled by permission of his people. The Germans were fierce, intrepid warriors who gave no quarter nor took none.

Lesson 3

The Huns were not merely a disorganized barbarian mob. They were ably led by Attila and were a very capable, organized war machine. They won every battle they ever fought and rarely took prisoners!

Lesson 4

Attila respected the power of the Christian church and recognized the value of a neutral ally at his rear when he moved into and conquered Eastern Europe.

Lesson 5

Cossacks were mostly from Ukraine and of Tatar descent. Cossacks were fierce warriors who lived in Eastern Europe and southern Russia. Cossacks were nomadic food gatherers and never connected with other people groups to form a nation state. Poorly inhabited and without efficient administration, their territories attracted potential conquerors. Eventually the Cossacks united to oppose the Tatars. The Cossacks were a match for all invaders. Since Poland maintained small forces on the borderlands, the Cossacks were often the only defenders for Ukraine against Tatar raids.

Chapter 22

Lesson 1

Bread is the central symbol of many religions. Jesus said, "I am the bread of life." Unleavened bread in Judaism became symbolic in many ways, including the Passover. The sharing of bread and salt is a traditional basis of hospitality and creates a usually unbreakable mutual obligation of protection.

Lesson 2

Hammurabi employed dogs to fight alongside his most elite Sumerian warriors.

The Greeks had special K-9 units at the Battle of Marathon. Man's best friend was present at every fortress siege in the Peloponnesian Wars. Later, the Celts, a Briton native group, bred fearsome war dogs, but were promptly copied by the Romans who did one better and created huge, ferocious Mastiffs that literally devoured Roman enemies. During the Middle Ages, Great Danes were used to jump onto the backs of horses, throwing the rider off, and allowing their master to kill the horseman. They were also used to scare horses and pursue fleeing enemies. In the New World, he 16th century conquistadors employed tactics not dissimilar to those of the Celts and Romans over a millennium earlier. Dressing their huge mastiffs in quilted overcoats, they were released into native villages, attacking the residents and wreaking havoc. They were also used to pursue and combat Aztec warriors at several battles.

Lesson 3

Answers will vary.

Lesson 4

Paper was in circulation but not preferred by anyone in the West. Invented in 105 AD in China, paper was at first kept secret, but the Arabs managed to learn the technique in the eighth century. With them it travelled to the areas of southern Europe under Arab dominion, most notably the southern the half of Iberia, and by the 12th — no later than the 13th century — western Europeans knew how to make paper. France initiated its own paper production in the 14th century, Germany in the 15th with England, the Low Countries and Scandinavia following subsequently. Paper was, in other words, readily available by the late Middle Ages, yet still parchment retained a high status, paper sometimes being regarded with outright disdain. Fortunately many historical documents were recorded on parchment, and thanks to its durability, these documents are available hundreds of years later.

Lesson 5

In the case of Charlemagne, it disarmed his enemies and caused them to underestimate him.

Chapter 23

Lesson 1

The United Kingdom was inhabited by English Native People groups: Celts, Picts, Scots, and Britons before the Romans came in AD 43. In fact, the rural areas of England were more populated in 100 B.C. than they are today! Roman control lasted for 400 years when the Romans withdrew for tactical reasons. They simply could not sustain these outposts in these remote parts of their kingdom. Nonetheless, the Roman influence was so pervasive and profound that Englishmen today point to the Roman occupation as their golden age. The Romans built the first roads and cities in England, many of which still exist today. The Anglo-Saxons then conquered the Britons and other indigenous people groups.

Lesson 2

Chesterton writes, "Rome itself, which had made all that strong world, was the weakest thing in it. The centre had been growing fainter and fainter, and now the centre disappeared. Rome had as much freed the world as ruled it, and now she could rule no more. Save for the presence of the Pope and his constantly increasing supernatural prestige, the eternal city became like one of her own provincial towns. A loose localism was the result rather than any conscious intellectual mutiny. There was anarchy, but there was no rebellion. For rebellion must have a principle, and therefore (for those who can think) an authority. Gibbon called his great pageant of prose The Decline and Fall of the Roman Empire. The Empire did decline, but it did not fall. It remains to this hour." Chesterton argues that the Roman Empire, in all its enduring influence, still affects world history today.

Lesson 3

The Domesday Book was the record of the great survey of England completed in 1086, executed for William the Conqueror. The survey was similar to a census by a government of today and is England's earliest surviving public records document. It is, in effect, the first social history of England.

Lesson 4

Magna Carta was the first document forced onto an English King by a group of his subjects, the feudal barons, in an attempt to limit his powers by law and protect their privileges. It was preceded and directly influenced by the Charter of Liberties in 1100, in which King Henry I had specified particular areas wherein his powers would be limited. The charter was an important part of the extensive historical process that led to the rule of constitutional law in the English speaking world. Wherever Englishmen went they carried their sense of law and justice with them. Perhaps no document has had more impact on English speaking people than the Magna Carta!

Lesson 5

According to Pyle, medieval England liked heroes who were strong, brave, but compassionate. No archer ever lived that could speed a gray goose shaft with such skill and cunning as his . . .

Chapter 24:

Lesson 1

Answers will vary.

Lesson 2

Answers will vary.

Lesson 3

Olasky warns that the differences between Christianity are too great to be ignored. They are not the same substance with different emphasizes. "It is neither wise nor compassionate to remain uninformed about those fiery religious rulings, and whether they have a basis in the Quran. Nor is it wise, when one culture may be threatening another, to settle for the most superficial coverage of that culture's belief, or to assume that both cultures have essentially the same understanding of who God is."

Lesson 4

This reader does not agree. Ms. Carter is terribly naïve. Answers will vary.

Lesson 5

While many Muslims adapted to the fast-paced changes common to Western industrialization and modernization, some Muslims rejected them. Instead, they created a rigid ideology imbedded in the traditional values and laws of the Koran. This is the phenomenon known today as Islamic fundamentalism, or Islamism. Islamism came to be seen as a struggle to return to the glorious days when Islam reigned supreme. It represents a yearning for the "pure" Islam as practiced by the prophet. Not unlike the American Quakers, the movement rejects much that is innovative. Islamists, however, take the rejection of modernity a step further. They perceive those who have introduced these innovations (the West) as its enemy and sought to destroy them.

Chapter 25

Lesson 1

An important Caliph was Uthman. When he died in AD 656, Muhammad's extended family claimed leadership of the Islamic world. Later a new leader named Muawiyah, unrelated to Muhammad, became Caliph and greatly expanded the Islamic state. A majority of Islamic people accepted his rule and this marked the beginning of the Umayyad Dynasty. This group referred to themselves as the Sunni. They comprised the majority of Islamic people. A very vocal, and powerful, if small in number, minority emerged too. They called themselves Shiites. There have been conflicts between these groups ever since.

Lesson 2

The main military threat of the Islamic army was the horse archer. As a light cavalry, the horse archers that made up the bulk of the Islamic armies were highly mobile. This mobility was used in four ways, which gave the Umayyads an advantage over their enemies. The predominance of the horse archer allowed the Islamic Army generally to control the place and timing of the major confrontations. The horse archers themselves could loose their arrows from the saddle without halting or dismounting, and even shoot backwards while in retreat. Islamic archers, moving, and shooting, would often, with great success, kill their opponents' horses.

Lesson 3

The Abbasids produced one of the greatest civilizations the world has ever known. While Europe wallowed in the mire of the Dark Ages, the Abbasids produced advances in science, mathematics, literature, medicine, architecture, religion as well as many other fields of discipline. Islamic cities such as Baghdad were the premier centers of learning and folks flocked there from all over the world to study. The Arab surgeon Abu al-Qasim pioneered surgical techniques that were used until the 20th century. He wrote the first illustrated surgical textbook. Beautifully illustrated with calligraphy, thousands of decorative scrolls were written by Islamic scholars. They developed the art of arabesque, in which intricate geometric designs were created for religious decoration.

Lesson 4

Ottoman foreign policy was never determined by religion. Never in their history were the Ottomans a crusading state or a theocracy. Relationship of the Ottoman state with Islam was essentially the same as any other empire's relationship with its official ideology. For the Ottomans, Islam was always the way to justify their policies, both foreign and domestic. They were never exclusively an Islamic state.

Lesson 5

There were no significant differences. Islam and Christianity (at that time) was a very male-centered, male-dominated religion. In fact, single Islam women had more rights than Christian women. In Islam a woman, married or single, is seen as a person in her own right, not merely as an adjunct to her husband. Children in the Islamic Empire and in Christian communities were treated like little adults. They were clothed the same as adults and expected to perform helpful functions in the home. Females in both cultures never went to school, but they worked at home taking care of their brothers and sisters and cooking. Often women did most of the domestic work. Females carried water from the well, and they went out to look for fuel for the fire. Young mean usually worked in the fields, plowing or weeding. Wealthier male children went to school where they learned to recite the Koran, or, in Christian schools, Roman Catholic Cataclysms.

Chapter 26

Lesson 1

Geography has had a great impact on Spanish history. The Pyrenees Mountains in the North has been an impediment to European involvement. The close proximity to Africa across the Strait of Gibraltar drew Spain into African politics. Its deep water warm ports encouraged Spain to be a seafaring nation. Spanish climate is a Mediterranean climate, characterized by dry and warm summers. Only in the Pyrenees would one find harsher, colder climates.

Lesson 2

In the era of exploration, discovery, and colonization, Spain accumulated tremendous wealth and a vast colonial empire through the conquest of Mexico by several conquistadors. The Spanish monarchy became for a time the most powerful in the world. In 1588, Philip II sent his Armada to invade England, but its destruction paved the way for the English Empire to emerge. Spain then sank rapidly to the status of a second-rate power and it never again played a major role in European politics. Why? The decline began with the destruction of the Armada. Then it continued with defeats in expensive foreign wars. The War of the Spanish Succession (1701–1714) resulted in Spain's loss of Belgium, Luxembourg, Milan, Sardinia, and Naples. Its colonial empire in the Americas vanished too. Lost as a result of English invasions of Spanish territory. By the end of the 17th century, Spain was a second-rate European power.

Lesson 3

The Islamic African Moors ruled in most of Spain from AD 710 until the late 1400's. The Moors had a significant impact on European cultural, socio-economic and political institutions. In 46 BC, the Roman army entered West Africa where they encountered black Africans whom they called 'Maures' from the Greek adjective mauros, meaning dark or black. The Moors were the African people who occupied northwest Africa, or present-day Morocco and Mauritania. These same African people became converts to Islam in the seventh century.

Spain was conquered not by Arabs, but by armies of Moors led by Arabs. The truth is that the conquest of the Iberian Peninsula, Spain and Portugal was an African not an Arab conquest. The conquest of Spain and Portugal in the eighth century, and later the greater part of Western Europe, was orchestrated by the Arabs who conquered North Africa; but the actual conquest was carried out by African adherents of Islam.

Lesson 4

Europe could have emerged as an Islamic nation! It is unlikely that Christopher Columbus would have discovered the New World.

Lesson 5

The language (diction) and syntax (sentence) clearly is anti-Catholic. Immediately after the conquest of Granada, in which these cruel and destructive habits were openly displayed, an occasion presented itself for giving still greater scope to their exercise. The subjugation of the Continent discovered by Columbus was a war of religion no less than of ambition and of conquest.

Chapter 27

Lesson 1

The Middle Ages have been called the "Dark Ages" because of the paucity of cultural offerings; however, such an appellation is at best ungenerous, at worst, inaccurate.

Lesson 2

The duty of a Middle Ages knight to learn how to fight and so serve their liege Lord according to the Code of Chivalry. The Code of Chivalry dictated that knights must be fearless in battle but would also cultured and generous in character. Knights must be ambidextrous and must be able to wield a two-handed sword, battle axe, mace, dagger and lance. A knight guarded the castle and supported his liege lord. Indeed, chivalry also demanded that the knight guard the church and, in general, the innocent and helpless. The knight, then, were the police, the army, and the farmer, all contained in one group.

Lesson 3

Islamic leaders represented Allah and assumed his prerogatives. Western leaders did not dare assume such grandiose positions.

Lesson 4

Feudalism brought order out of chaos. While some of the gentry was pernicious, and even cruel, by and large, the gentry were decent. All involved benefited from this most stratified of European societies in all of history.

Lesson 5

Answers will vary.

Chapter 28

Lesson 1

Answers will vary.

Lesson 2

Women in all ages, at this time, had no voting privileges, and without exception, could own no property. Only in Mesopotamia was it illegal to physically to abuse women. At least in Christian medieval Europe, women could expect their husband to be faithful. Monogamy was expected. In other cultures women had to be faithful to husbands but the reverse was not true.

Lesson 3

Viking invasions were a major factor in the development of cities during the early Middle Ages. To protect themselves from marauding Vikings, villages erected walls. This led to the great medieval walled cities. These walled cities became known as "bourgs," "burghs," and later, boroughs. Inhabitants were known as bourgeois. By the mid-900s, these fortified towns filled the European landscape from the Mediterranean as far north as Hamburg, Germany.

Lesson 4

Clearly medieval life is like life anywhere: full of ordinary conflicts and resolutions. Richard Fette was caught accepting stolen goods. "Richard Fette in mercy for receiving sheaves in autumn upon the delivery of the reeve against the prohibition of the steward; pledge, the whole villa." Poor Agnes Maud will be unmarried for awhile. "Agnes Maud's daughter at the instance of her friends gives the lord 12 d. for permission to marry; she gives no more because she is very poor." And so forth.

Lesson 5

It was a difficult time for people to make a living but harried people, with their eyes on Heaven more than the hardships down below, found solace and inspiration that encouraged them to express themselves in the arts.

Chapter 29

Lesson 1

Medieval peasants ate mostly bread. It was their main staple. The best-harvested wheat went exclusively to the market, or to the castle. Peasant breads were made from barley and rye, baked into dark heavy loaves. Rich gentry drank wine; peasants drank beer. No one wanted to drink water — it was generally unhealthy and no one knew to boil it first. Pottage, a thick soup, was often favored over bread for any meal, because it required grains that were not very valuable. Peasants ate the same thing for breakfast and supper and almost never ate any lunch.

Lesson 2

If it was serious enough, the priest would be asked to pray over the poor sick person. If that did not work, the barber might be asked to bleed the patient.

Lesson 3

Among knights and gentry, hungry for intrigue, romance and love became an imagined vocation. Courtly love became the subject of some of the most famous medieval poems and early paintings. Romantic stories of courtly love were spread throughout medieval Europe by troubadours and minstrels. The language used by this new poetry was intended to be sung, played on musical instruments brought back from the crusades. This was a new style of expressive writing.

Lesson 4

At dawn the watchman blew a blast on his bugle to awaken the castle. After a Spartan breakfast of bread and wine or beer, the nobles attended mass in the castle chapel. The lord then would hold court, functioning as judge, advocate, general, and counselor for all his fiefdom. The lady of the castle inspected the work of her large staff of servants. She saw that her spinners, weavers, and embroiderers furnished clothes for the castle and rich vestments for the clergy. She and her ladies also helped to train the pages. Sometime between 9 a.m. and noon, a trumpet summoned the lord's household to the great hall for what they called dinner and what we would call lunch. They gustily ate huge quantities of rich food. In winter the ill-preserved meat smacked fierily of East Indian spices, bought at enormous cost to hide the rank taste. Great, flat pieces of bread called trenchers served as plates and, after the meal, were flung to the dogs around the table or given to the poor. Huge pies, or pasties, filled with several kinds of fowl or fish, were relished. Metal or wood cups or leather "jacks" held cider, beer, or wine. Coffee and tea were not used in Europe until after the Middle Ages. Supper which, unless it was a very special affair, was served soon after dark. Lighting made this difficult, so it was a simple affair. Shortly after sunset, most of the household was in bed and fast asleep.

Lesson 5

Each family lived in a dark, dank hut made of wood or wicker daubed with mud and thatched with straw or rushes. Layers of straw or reeds covered the floor, fouled by the pigs, chickens, and other animals housed with the family. The one bed was a pile of dried leaves or straw. All slept in their rough garb, with skins of animals for cover. Whole families shared one bed. A cooking fire of peat or wood burned drearily day and night in a clearing on the dirt floor. The smoke seeped out through a hole in the roof or the open half of a two-piece door. Nobody built chimneys. The only furniture was a plank table on trestles, a few stools, perhaps a chest, and probably a loom for the women to make their own cloth. Every hut had a vegetable patch.

Chapter 30

Lesson 1

Charlemagne was a smart and an ambitious king, aggressive and ruthless. He was not a great military tactician, but he was a stubborn campaigner and was often able to wear the enemy down through sheer force. He rode as commander at the head of at least half of them. He moved his armies over wide reaches of country with unbelievable speed, but every move was planned in advance. Schools had all but disappeared in the 8th century under the rule of Charles Martel, Charlemagne's grandfather. Charlemagne, in spite of

his illiteracy, valued education and promoted it through his reign. Most of all, though, Charlemagne was a very committed Christian believer. His devotion to the church became the great driving force of his remarkable life.

Lesson 2

The Roman Catholic Church during the Middle Ages had no significant army so it relied on secular rulers to protect it. Charlemagne travels to Rome in 800 to support the pope. Pope Leo III crowns Charlemagne as the new Roman Emperor, the king of the Holy Roman Empire. Charlemagne knew that the legal emperor was undoubtedly in Byzantium Constantinople. Nevertheless this public alliance between the pope and the ruler of a confederation of Germanic tribes now reflects the reality of political power in the west. And it launches the concept of the new Holy Roman Empire which will play an important role throughout the Middle Ages. The confusion between ecclesiological and secular authority will continue for several centuries, but for now, the Holy Roman Empire brought much needed stability and peace to Central Europe.

Lesson 3

Medieval education can be understood better if one realizes that for thousands of years childhood as it is known today literally did not exist. No psychological distinction was made between child and adult. The medieval school was not really intended for children. Rather, it was a kind of vocational school for clerks and clergymen. In Greece education was similar, although much more emphasis was placed on physical activity.

Lesson 4

He was very forward in succoring the poor, and in that gratuitous generosity which the Greeks call alms, so much so that he not only made a point of giving in his own country and his own kingdom, but when he discovered that there were Christians living in poverty in Syria, Egypt, and Africa, at Jerusalem, Alexandria, and Carthage, he had compassion on their wants, and used to send money over the seas to them. The reason that he zealously strove to make friends with the kings beyond seas was that he might get help and relief to the Christians living under their rule. He cherished the Church of St. Peter the Apostle at Rome above all other holy and sacred places, and heaped its treasury with a vast wealth of gold, silver, and precious stones (Einhard).

Lesson 5

Moreover, the study of the sources enables us to some extent to form our own opinions of the past, so that we need not rely entirely upon mere manuals, which are always one, and generally two or three, removes from the sources themselves. When we get at the sources themselves we no longer merely read and memorize; we begin to consider what may be safely inferred from the statements before us and so. develop the all-important faculty of criticism. We are not simply accumulating facts but are attempting to determine their true nature and meaning (Robinson).

Chapter 31

Lesson 1

With its own laws, lands and taxes the Catholic Church was a very powerful, wealthy institution. The Catholic Church also imposed taxes. Opposition to the Catholic Church would result in excommunication. This meant that the person who was excommunicated could not attend any church services, receive the sacraments and would go straight to hell when they died. This was a very ominous treat to all medieval people.

Lesson 2

I think the church of the Middle Ages did very well! The church sent courageous, godly men and women to all the areas of the world and made a great difference.

Lesson 3

The Church understood and still understands that God is in control of all. The Church was a stimulus for generating new innovative ideals. It was an obstacle to progress.

Lesson 4

The church was the medieval society, and, by and large, loved by all its people. Why not make the church building higher than any castle?

Lesson 5

Actually the roles were very similar. Medieval parsons lived and died among their people. They did not enjoy any particular advantage. Bishops and other church officials, also, by and large, served the people with integrity and generosity.

Chapter 32

Lesson 1

We are forgiven as we forgive. And forgive us our debts, as we also have forgiven our debtors (Matt. 6:12) (Mark 11:25).

Lesson 2

As God is love, the poet becomes love, as she loves God. Her longing causes her to love God more intensely. And she will love God forever!

Lesson 3

Answers will vary.

Lesson 4

Answers will vary.

Lesson 5

Answers will vary.

Chapter 33

Lesson 1

The Crusades that were launched on the holy land, from Pope Urban II's speech at the council of Clermont in 1095 to the siege and conquest of Jerusalem by the Crusaders in 1099, initiated a new phase of relationship between the West and Islamic peoples. The expressed purpose of the Crusades was to free the Holy Land from the infidel. It pretty was conducted that way, with many excesses of course.

Lesson 2

It is a nice ideal but I doubt it still exists.

Lesson 3

Heroes must be brave, kind, and, above all, principled.

Lesson 4

Unfortunately, these mercenary groups, with the most laudable of motivations, can forget that good must overcome evil. That is the cause of Christ!

Lesson 5

The Crusades failed to achieve their specific objective; they permanently changed the complexion of world history. On the contrary, their influence extended over a much wider geographical field than just the Holy Land. Much of the crusading fervor carried over to the fight against the Moors in Spain and the Slavs in Eastern Europe. Politically the Crusades weakened the Byzantine Empire and accelerated its fall. Although the early Crusades strengthened the authority of the papacy in Europe, the bad performance of the later crusades, weakened both the crusading ideal and respect for the papacy. Contact with the East widened the scope of the Europeans, ended their isolation, and exposed them to an admirable civilization. Although it is easy to exaggerate the economic effects of the crusades, they did influence the reopening of the eastern

Mediterranean to Western commerce, which itself had an effect on the rise of cities and the emergence of a hard money economy in the West. http://history-world.org/mainmenu.htm

Chapter 34

Lesson 1

In the exploration and exploitation of the New World, Spain found an outlet for the crusading energies that the war against the Muslims had stimulated. New discoveries and conquests came in quick succession. Vasco Nunez de Balboa reached the Pacific in 1513, and the survivors of Ferdinand Magellan's expedition completed the circumnavigation of the globe in 1522. In 1519 the conquistador Hernando Cortes subdued the Aztecs in Mexico with a handful of followers, and between 1531 and 1533 Francisco Pizzaro overthrew the empire of the Incas and established Spanish dominion over Peru. By the end of the reign of Ferdinand and Isabella, Spain was a first-rate power in the European world.

Lesson 2

In America, there was Cahokia. One mound, located across the Mississippi River from St. Louis, is larger than the Great Pyramid in Egypt. Its base covered 14 acres and it rose in four terraces to 100 feet. Other answers may vary.

Lesson 3

Columbus's idea of sailing west to get to the east was not original with him, nor did he ever claim that it was. Columbus drew upon science and knowledge accumulated over thousands of years. Columbus's ideas of the distance between Europe and Asia were based on the descriptions contained in several reputable geographic works. In fact, most educated Europeans were sure that the world was much smaller than it really is.

Lesson 4

Apparently, Columbus is already suspicious that he has not reached the East Indies. Furthermore, the natives could never provide the amount of gold that he desired. Still, as he put it, "They willingly traded everything they owned. They do not bear arms, and do not know them, for I showed them a sword, they took it by the edge and cut themselves out of ignorance. With fifty men we could subjugate them all and make them do whatever we want."

Lesson 5

I really think Columbus was motivated to advance the Kingdom of God. Of course, he understood the necessity to find gold and other valuables, but these were less important to Columbus than they were to others. Historian Valery Flint states: "The debate about Columbus ' character and achievements began at least as early as the first rebellion of the Taino Indians and continued with Roldán, Bobadilla, and Ovando. It has been revived periodically (notably by Las Casas and Jean-Jacques Rousseau) ever since. The Columbus quincentenary of 1992 rekindled the intensity of this early questioning and redirected its aims, often profitably. The word "encounter" is now preferred to "discovery" when describing the contacts between the Old World and the New, and more attention has come to be paid to the fate of the Native American peoples and to the sensibilities of non-Christians. Enlightening discoveries have been made about the diseases that reached the New World through Columbus' agency as well as those his sailors took back with them to the Old. The pendulum may, however, now have swung too far. Columbus has been made a whipping boy for events far beyond his own reach or knowledge and a means to an agenda of condemnation that far outstrips his own guilt. Thus, too little attention has recently been paid to the historical circumstances that conditioned him. His obsessions with lineage and imperialism, his seemingly bizarre Christian beliefs, and his apparently brutal behavior come from a world remote from that of modern democratic ideas, it is true; but it was the world to which he belonged. The forces of European expansion, with their slaving and search for gold, had been unleashed before him and were at his time quite beyond his control. Columbus simply decided to be in the vanguard of them. He succeeded. Columbus' towering stature as a seaman and navigator, the sheer power of his religious convictions (self-delusory as they sometimes were), his personal magnetism, his courage, his endurance, his determination, and, above all, his achievements as an explorer, should continue to be recognized." Valerie I.J. Flint: G.F. Grant Professor of History, University of Hull , England. Author of *The Imaginative Landscape of Christopher Columbus*.

Chapter 1 Exam Options

Option 1 – Matching:

1. Civilization: A highly developed, sustaining society.
2. Antediluvian: Time before the Great Flood.
3. Mesopotamia: The area approximately between and around the Tigris and Euphrates Rivers.
4. Sumer: The first significant civilization group in Mesopotamia.
5. Hammurabi Code: The first written, rule of law, in the world.
6. Agrarian Societies: People groups whose main livelihood is farming.
7. Nomadic Societies: People groups whose main livelihood is farming.
8. Monotheism: A religion that worships one god.
9. Polytheism: A religion that worships many gods.
10. Marduk: A significant Babylonian god.

Option 2 – Essay:

Though answers will vary, I would place my village on a hill (620) close to the river. It would be both defensible and close to water sources. Surrounding this hill is relatively flat, delta, farm land. If I needed to irrigate my crops, I could draw from the river.

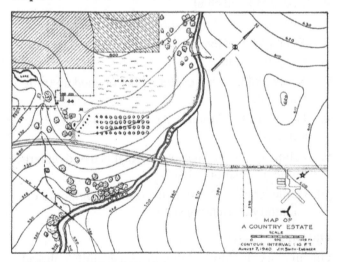

Chapter 2 Exam Options

Option 1 – Matching:

1. Old Kingdom: The Old Kingdom, arising after the Great Flood, developed a strong national government—the first in history.
2. Middle Kingdom: There were several civil wars and King Mentuhotep II united the Kingdom again but he moved the capital to Thebes.
3. New Kingdom: It was in the New Kingdom, probably during the reign of Ramses II, that Moses took his people from Egypt to the Promised Land.
4. Delta: Fertile lowlands near the mouth of a river.
5. Black Land: Fertile loam soil.
6. Red Land: Arid, dry land, usually rich in iron ore.
7. Pharaoh: King/leader of Egypt.
8. Oligarchy: A government whose leadership is one strong leader.
9. Despot: A tertiary, omnipotent, usually malevolent leader.
10. Totalitarian: A government where total control is lodged in one leader.

Option 2 – Essay:

Christianity with its emphasis on the rule of law fulfilled through the fulfillment of the covenant of grace has insured a viable Christian civilization for centuries. It is not the only viable civilization, nor is it superior (although we serve the one true God), but it has encouraged a sustaining, moral civilization that has benefited the whole world and all of world history.

Chapter 3 Exam Options

Option 1 – Matching:

1. Abraham: The father patriarch of Judaism.
2. Israel: Another name for Jacob, the name of the Jewish state.
3. Canaan: The Promised Land, the land promised to the Jewish people.
4. Exodus: The liberation of the Jewish people from bondage in Egypt.
5. Diaspora: After the destruction of the Temple (AD 70), the Jewish people spread all over the world.
6. Zionist: Radical Jewish thought that wishes to form a Jewish state.
7. Kubbutzim: Communal living groups in Israel.
8. Wadis: Mainly dry water courses.
9. Judges: Leaders of Israel during a period of great stress in Israeli history.
10. Judicial, Legislative, Executive: Three different branches of government.

Option 2 – Essay:

Certainly vilification from Islamic hotheads hurt efforts at peace. But the fact remains: the creation of Israel displaced a people who really do need a homeland (Palestinians). If this can be solved, perhaps there will be peace in the Middle East. Answers will vary.

Chapter 4 Exam Options

Option 1 – Matching:

1. Harrappan: First people group to reach India.
2. Marketplace: Place where commerce occurs.
3. Vedas: Hindu sacred texts.
4. Polytheists: Religion that worships many gods.
5. Ramayana: An ancient Hindu Sanskrit epic.
6. Panchatantra: Ancient Indian beast fables.
7. Guru: Religious teacher.
8. Gandharva Vivaha: Love marriage.
9. Saris: Woman's garment.
10. Castes: Hindu social class.

Option 2 – Essay:

There is much debate about this issue. This reader is unsure; however, most historians feel that Sumer (Mesopotamia) originated first. The first civilization appeared around 5,000 BC. A civilization is defined as "An advanced state of intellectual, cultural, and material development in human society, marked by progress in the arts and sciences, the extensive use of record-keeping, including writing, and the appearance of complex political and social institution" (American Heritage Dictionary). The first civilization that fits this definition is the city states of Mesopotamia, located between the Tigris and Euphrates rivers in present-day Iraq. Closely following these city states in Mesopotamia was the culture of ancient Egypt on the river Nile. And finally, the Indus River civilization in India, which developed around the same time that Egypt, began to expand their sphere of influence.

Chapter 5 Exam Options

Option 1 – Matching:

1. Yellow River: The Yellow River or Huang He, formerly known as the Hwang Ho, is the second-longest river in China. It is the location of many ancient Chinese people groups.
2. Class System: Division among people groups according to special criteria.
3. Oriental Monarch: An Eastern autocrat, monarch, who is usually more despotic than Western types.
4. Confucius: Early Chinese philosopher.
5. Calligraphy: Decorative writing.

6. Mandarins: A Chinese people type.
7. Conscripted: Forced to serve for a purpose.
8. Feudal System: Hierarchical system based on patronage.
9. Zhing He: Famous Chinese naval captain.
10. Galloping Horse Ships: Description of massive Chinese vessels.

Option 2 – Essay:

The European powers, practicing mercantilism, exploited the New World and Native peoples and did so with no pang of conscience. In fact, many European settlers felt it was their moral and religious obligation to do so. Zeng He and his Chinese superiors, on the other hand, did not wish to exploit, nor did they wish to benefit from, they wanted to seduce the world into their fold! The truth is, it has always been an ancient Chinese trait: they were so enamored with their won culture that they simply knew others would be too!

Chapter 6 Exam Options

Option 1 – Matching:

1. Empire: Lands ruled by single authority.
2. Mongol: People group coming from the Mongolian Steppes, conquered China.
3. Tatars: Central Asian Warlike people; absorbed by Mongols.
4. Khan: Mongol chief.
5. Genghis Khan: First major leader of the Mongols.
6. Kublai Khan: Greatest Mongol chief, grandson of Genghis Kahn.
7. Marco Polo: Italian explorer who opened up trade with China.
8. Domesticated Animals: As opposed to wild animals.
9. Labor Intensive: An economy that is based on large numbers of labor workers.
10. Confederation: A loose government composed of voluntary consenting states.

Option 2 – Essay:

One may see the Mongol Empire as a gigantic political force, bringing almost the entire continent of Asia under the control of one great Khan. The Mongol government was a superior one, and thus the whole continent became interconnected. During the Mongol Empire, one was guaranteed safety in travel throughout the entire empire. Thus, the empire created a huge economical boom and a great exchange of culture and knowledge throughout the entire world. As a result of the Mongol conquests, the Silk Road was reopened and the route from Europe to Asia was no longer thought to be impassable. A great deal of knowledge reached Europe, including art, science, and gunpowder; which greatly contributed in bringing western Europe out of the dark ages. Likewise, in Asia, we saw an exchange of ideas between Persia and China. Asia, and Asia Minor, experienced an unprecedented era of peace that stimulated commerce and growth. (Peter Stearns, World History in Brief)

Chapter 7 Exam Options

Option 1 – Matching:

1. Daimyo: Japanese feudal lord.
2. Bakufu: Shogun commander.
3. Tokugawa Period: Important period of Japanese history where Japan was ruled by shoguns.
4. Meiji Period: A Japanese era which extended from September 1868 through July 1912.
5. Shoguns: Japanese leader.
6. Tertiary Leaders: Leaders who are important, but not at the center of the action.
7. Japanese Feudalism: Japanese hierarchical government based on patronage.
8. Guilds: Professional organizations.
9. Sakoku: Foreign relations policy that forbid outsiders from entering Japan.
10. Commodore Matthew Perry: The American who opened trade to China.

Option 2 – Essay:

Egypt was isolated, but not by choice. There were significant physical barriers — a desert, a sea, and a mountain range — that separated Egypt from other people groups. However, there was no systematic government policy to create this isolation. It simply was a geographical necessity. Sakoku was the foreign relations policy of Japan under which no foreigner could enter nor could any Japanese leave the country on penalty of death. The policy remained in effect until 1853 with the arrival of Commodore Matthew Perry and the opening of Japan.

Chapter 8 Exam Options

Option 1 – Matching:

1. Omniscient: Divinely present everywhere.
2. Omnipotent: Divinely in control everywhere.
3. Avesta: Sacred texts of Zoroastrianism.

4. Conversion: Total change to a new status or allegiance.
5. Humanism: A philosophy that places mankind at the center of the discussion.
6. Atheism: A belief that there is no god.
7. Meditation: To reflect on life and truth.
8. Wu Wei: A concept of Taoism: knowing when to act and when not to act.
9. Laozi: The founder of Taoism.
10. Hinduism: A polytheistic, animistic religion.

Option 2 – Essay:

One historian argues, "The decline of the classical empires contributed several ingredients to the spread of what turned out to be the great world religions. Previously, most religion had been regional. Buddhism, spreading through India at various points in the classical period, could embrace a whole subcontinent. As Hinduism evolved from the Brahman religion, it did the same and also spread to a few other areas of Indian commercial influence in Southeast Asia. Christianity showed an ability to win a growing minority in the Roman Empire and at a few points beyond its borders, in the Middle East and North Africa. The waning of the great empires so confused and reshuffled geographical boundaries, from the Mediterranean to the Pacific, that the regional confines of religion were modified more dramatically. The same political decline encouraged people to turn to more spiritual institutions and rewards. The result was one of the world's key periods in which beliefs shifted and cultural allegiances took on new territorial patterns. Even religions still essentially regional, such as Daoism in China and Hinduism in India, worked to win new levels of active popular adherence. Just as the fifth century BC had clustered the origins of major philosophical systems for the educated elites in China and the Mediterranean, so the period A.D. 200–700 grouped fundamental changes in religious alignments." http://history-world.org/

Chapter 9 Exam Options

Option 1 – Matching:

Fill in the blanks with words from the following list:

1. Hellas: Greece.
2. Mycenaeans: Cultural period in ancient Greece.
3. Iliad: Homer's epic classic about the siege of Troy.
4. Odyssey: Homer's epic classic about Odysseus' return from Troy.
5. Alexander: Alexander the Great conquered most of the known world.

6. Aeneas: The founder of Rome, survivor of Troy.

7. Battle of Thermopylae: Where the Spartan 300 stopped the Persian army for two days.

8. King Leonidas: King of the Spartan 300.

9. Marathon: A Greek messenger ran approximately 26 miles to Athens to tell his superiors that the Persians were defeated. He died afterwards.

10. Democracy: Government by the people.

Option 2 – Essay:

Geographical factors played an important part in shaping the events of Greek history. The numerous mountain ranges that crisscross the peninsula, which is about the size of Georgia, led to the development of fiercely independent city-states and the failure of the Greeks to unite into a single state. The indented coastline and the many islands offshore stimulated seagoing trade, and the rocky soil (less than a fifth of Greece can be cultivated) and few natural resources encouraged the Greeks to establish colonies abroad. All these things they did — built city-states, navies, founded colonies, and farmed on all the land that they had.

Chapter 10 Exam Options

Option 1 – Matching:

1. Pathos: In literature, pathos is the "heart" or "spirit" of a literary work.

2. Renaissance: Classical revival at the end of the Middle Ages.

3. Classical: Traditional.

4. Hellenistic: Greek.

5. Greek Enlightenment: A time of significant artistic production.

6. Satyr Plays: Greek tragic comedies.

7. Didactic: Artistic genres that teach a lesson.

8. Aristotelian Tradition: Tradition of using the Socratic dialogue and the didactic.

9. Poetics: Aristotle's book discussing poetry.

10. Motif: Theme.

Option 2 – Essay:

Americans in the near future will be looking to places of stability and strength for direction. By default, those people whose lives are in reasonably good shape (i.e., born-again Christians), who have some reason to live beyond the next paycheck will have an inexorable appeal. That is good news for Christians. Millions of new godly, spirit-filled leaders will be emerging in the next 20 years. For instance, around 1/12 of the new

graduate/leaders of our universities may be Christians homeschoolers. Can the reader imagine what it will mean to a culture to suddenly have 3 or 4 million spirit-filled, stable Christian leaders coming forth into the nation? There has not been a more potentially ameliorating cultural possibility than the time when Augustine and his generation led his nation at the end of the Roman Empire. The barbarians conquered the Roman Empire; the Christians conquered (culturally) the barbarians.

Chapter 11 Exam Options

Option 1 – Matching:

1. Byzantium: The Eastern Roman Empire.

2. Darius III: Persian king.

3. Persepolis: Persepolis was the ceremonial capital of the Achaemenid Empire (ca. 550–330 BC).

4. Hellenistic: Greek in nature.

5. Alexandria: Famous Egyptian/Greek city.

6. Ptolemy: Alexander's top general.

7. Pharos Island: Island off Alexander. Housed the Pharos light house.

8. Septuagint: Greek version of the Old Testament.

9. Octavian: The first Roman emperor.

10. Origen: Early church father.

Option 2 – Essay:

Alexander the Great was an important man who influenced many lives, but he was not a true history maker. Moses was a history maker. In Deuteronomy 34:1–4 Moses has come to the end of his life. He will not go into the Promised Land. He knew by Exodus 3 that he was not going in. But Moses was a history maker. He understood that history is made by people who obey God, not by those who have power and influence. History makers assert the raw rule of God in the historical. History makers have an omnipotent God. Not an anemic, Ahab-like God, who exists to satisfy whines and whims. Not a Rotarian God. He is a jealous powerful God. Our culture, and the culture in which Alexander lived, promulgated a delusion of immortality with no judgment. Our response to the struggles of life and the triumphs of life (as Alexander knew) should be like Jeremiah who said, "The word of the Lord came to me, saying: 'Buy for yourself my field which is at Anathoth, for you have the right of redemption to buy it, (Jeremiah's ancestor named Abiathar owned this land)," (Jeremiah 32:6–76). The funny thing is Jeremiah would never live on this land. He bought property for his future. He invested in what is not seen because God told him to do that. Alexander the Great would never do that. He conquered lands but changed no hearts.

Chapter 12 Exam Options

Option 1 – Matching:

1. Indigenous: Local people.
2. Plains of Latium: Where the Latin people-group originated.
3. Tiber River: River that runs through Rome.
4. Etruscans: The people group who lived in the area of Rome before the Latins invaded.
5. Phoenicians: A sea people in the Middle East.
6. Republic: A political entity with elected officials.
7. Romulus: One of the legendary founders of Rome.
8. Senate: The legislators of Rome.
9. Julius Caesar: The last leader of the republic.
10. Utilitarian: Things that are practical and useful.

Option 2 – Essay:

To murder one's friend, even in the name of justice, seems to be extreme and pushes "moral necessity" to the extreme. While the assassination of a notorious leader like Adolf Hitler seems desirable and necessary, the assassination of Julius Caesar, who had performed nothing other than proclaiming himself emperor, seems to be injudicious. There were other ways that the Republic could have been restored. In point of fact, the violent act inflicted on Julius Casear drove Rome even farther away from having a Republic. In fact, Rome was never to have a Republic again.

Chapter 13 Exam Options

Option 1 – Matching:

1. Messiah: The Savior of mankind.
2. Nazareth: The town where Jesus lived.
3. Rabbi: Spiritual leader of the Jewish community.
4. Deacons: A group who serves in the church.
5. Presbytery: Leadership group in the church.
6. Elders: The local church leaders.
7. Christian Worship Assembly: A term for an early church.
8. Epistles: Sacred letters in the church.
9. Gospels: Matthew, Mark, Luke, and John.
10. Didache: Writings about the early church that are not sacred.

Option 2 – Essay:

Answers will vary. The theologian Abraham Heschel reminds us that a prophet is a disturber of worldly peace. He/she comes to give peace, but "not as the world gives" Christ says (John 14:27). I preach Christ — crucified and resurrected. My Christ calls us all to faithful discipleship. Through Gospel messages and by my life example I invite my congregation to express their faith through a personal confession of commitment to Christ (i.e., being born again) and through a public commitment to bring justice into their part of the world. Isaac Watts' famous hymn, "When I Survey the Wondrous Cross," is the best summation of my theological perspective. "When I survey the wondrous cross on which the Prince of Glory died,/My riches gain I count but loss, And pour contempt on all my pride . . ." As the theologian Dietrich Bonhoeffer mused a few weeks before his death in a Nazi prison in late World War II, so I profess: Christ is at once my boundary and my rediscovered center. In my Resurrected Lord I see the faithfulness of a gracious God encountering sinful humankind. And how we need the grace of God! We are a lonely, separated, broken people desperately in need of a Savior. All humankind, good and bad alike, rich and poor, are in the wrong before God, and we all fall under God's judgment. In spite of our sincere intentions, we systematically, inevitably shatter our virtuous dreams by allowing self-interest and hostility to motivate our lives. Without the resurrected Lord at the center of our being, we are, as the Christian poet T. S. Eliot hauntingly reflects, "paralyzed force, gesture without motion." Yes, we all deserve the wrath of God. As the theologian Karl Barth explains, "The judgment of God is the righteousness of God without Jesus Christ." But, God, out of His great love for us all, gave us His Son to be our Savior. Yes, with Christ as the center of our lives, we have hope. The Church must be unequivocal and outspoken in its confession that a decision for Christ is the only way to health, happiness, wholeness, and eternal security. "Were the whole realm of nature mine, that were a present far too small; /Love so amazing, so divine, Demands my soul, my life, my all." God's love is so amazing that He went His only Begotten Son to die for us. Therefore He has a right now to demand all of us in return! The Church of Jesus Christ must be unambivalent in its confession that "there is neither Jew or Greek, there is neither slave or free person, there is neither male or female: for you are all one in Christ Jesus (Gals. 3:28). In the areas of social justice, equality between the sexes and races, ministry to the poor and to the homeless, peacemaking, the church must be prophetic. "For in as much as you helped the least of these, you helped me . . ." Equally important is the Church's responsibility to create and to support wholesome family life. The Christian family remains the single most important channel that God has chosen to inculcate in humankind His nurturing principles of fulfilled living. Solid, healthy Christian family life is a primary goal of my ministry. Recognizing the pressures of economics and time, the church must nonetheless equip parents of the 21st century with the knowledge and skills necessary to keep Jesus Christ in the center of our homes and therefore in the center of our society.

Chapter 14 Exam Options

Option 1 – Matching:

1. Spiritual Gifts: Gifts of the Holy Spirit were given to the Church, beginning at Pentecost, for the empowering of the Saints, and as an encouragement and helps.
2. Monotheistic: To believe in one God.
3. Apologists: Defenders of the Christian faith.
4. Systematic Church Dogma: Comprehensive church doctrine.
5. Church Fathers: Historical defenders of the faith.
6. Canon: The officially sanctioned books of the Bible.
7. Apocryphal: Debatable inter-testament books of the Bible.
8. Mennonite: Early, believer baptism, pacifist sect of Christianity.
9. Anabaptists: Believed in believer baptism.
10. Quakers: Had no clergy and liturgy.

Option 2 – Essay:

Indeed, until there were heretical Christian movements, no theology was necessary. Even pagan attacks could be handled with what the church had. But when there were "Christian" heretics, the Church had to define more clearly its corpus of Truth. At the core, the Church was about responding to the Holy Spirit. As one theologian explains, "The dominant idea in the Christian community, at the moment at which we are now arrived, was the coming of the Holy Spirit. People were believed to receive it in the form of a mysterious breath, which passed over the assembly. Every inward consolation, every bold movement, every flush of enthusiasm, every feeling of lively and pleasant gayety, which was experienced without knowing whence it came, was the work of the Spirit. These simple consciences referred, as usual, to some exterior cause the exquisite sentiments which were being created

in them. When all were assembled, and when they awaited in silence inspiration from on high, a murmur, any noise whatever, was believed to be the coming of the Spirit. In the early times, it was the apparitions of Jesus which were produced in this manner. Now the turn of ideas had changed. It was the divine breath which passed over the little Church, and filled it with a celestial effluvium. These beliefs were strengthened by notions drawn from the Old Testament. The prophetic spirit is represented in the Hebrew books as a breathing which penetrates man and inspires him. In the beautiful vision of Elijah, God passes by in the form of a gentle wind, which produces a slight rustling noise."

Chapter 15 Exam Options

Option 1 – Matching:

1. Barbarians: Germanic people who conquered the western portion of the Roman Empire.
2. Manichaeanism: A very popular 5th-century religion among intellectuals.
3. Cicero: Famous Roman orator.
4. Atonement: Sacrifice for sins.
5. Dualistic: A view that good and bad are equal in strength.
6. Exegesis: Analysis of Scripture.
7. Donatism: A sect of people who could not forgive apostate repenting Christians.
8. Pelagianism: An emphasis on free will.
9. Visigoth Alaric: Germanic barbarian tribes.
10. Hegemony: Political and cultural control.

Option 2 – Essay:

Answers will vary.

Chapter 16 Exam Options

Option 1 – Matching:

1. Ghana: Ancient West African nation.
2. Sahara Desert: A desert in northwest Africa.
3. Commodities: Goods and services that have economic value.
4. Mauritania: West African country.
5. Industrial State: Nations whose primary economic prosperity is tied to industries.
6. The Gold Coast: West African coastline that sold vast amounts of gold to Europeans.
7. Niger: An important West African river.
8. Sundjata: Founder of the Mali Empire.
9. Timbuktu: Famous African city.

10. Songhay: A people group who replaced the Malis.

Option 2 – Essay:

African civilizations until the 16th century compared favorably with those in Europe and Asia. Ethiopia, parts of Ghana, were thriving while the Roman Empire was disintegrating. In the tenth century, Timbuktu was trading by sea with Persia and India! Europeans hard knew they existed! After about A.D. 1200, when European states were becoming centralized monarchies, similar kingdoms were rising in Sub-Sahara Africa, particularly in regions drained by the Niger River. Europeans arriving after the 1400s found well-organized governments and societies bound by strong traditions.

Chapter 17 Exam Options

Option 1 – Matching:

1. Native Americans: Native, indigenous people groups in the Northern hemisphere of the Americas.
2. Mound Building: Native American burial mounds and large hills of dirt built, perhaps, to escape high water.
3. Cahokia Mounds: Spectacular mounds in Middle America.
4. Deforestation: Rapid and totally debilitating removal of forests from an area.
5. Shamans: Native American priests and religious leaders.
6. Matrilineal: To find one's identity from one's mother.
7. Sedentary hunters-gatherers: These are hunters who live in one place.
8. Kinship: To build ties and relationships around family ties.
9. Domicile: Place where one lives.
10. Patrilineal: Lineage from the father.

Option 2 – Essay:

It seems clear that, in most cultures agriculture is a major feature in determining the ability of societies to achieve the surplus production and complexity needed for those elements usually associated with civilization. With the adoption of agriculture and a sedentary way of life, the process of civilization was set in motion in the Americas.

Chapter 18 Exam Options

Option 1 – Matching:

1. Andes Mountains: A mountain range through southern South America.
2. Glaciers: Huge layers of ice.
3. Talismans: Religious charms.
4. Cosmology: Study of the supernatural.
5. Gypsum: White substance/mineral.
6. Functionality: Operational.
7. Aesthetics: Ideas of beauty.
8. Machu Pachacutec: Important Inca ruler.
9. Conquistadors: Spanish explorers.
10. Bureaucracy: Administrative system.

Option 2 – Essay:

Historian Michael Adas writes, "The Olmecs have been called the 'mother civilization' of South America. Maize cultivation, especially along the rivers, provided the basis for a state ruled by a hereditary elite and in which the ceremonialism of a complex religion dominated much of life. At about the time that Tutankhamen ruled in Egypt, the Olmec civilization flourished in South America. The Olmecs remain a mystery. Some of their monumental sculptures seem to bear Negroid features; others appear to be representations of humans with feline attributes. They were great carvers of jade and traded or conquered to obtain it. They developed a numerical system — based on 20 — and a calendar that combined a 365-day year with a 260-day ritual cycle. This became the basis of all South American calendar systems. What language they spoke and what became of their civilization remain unknown, but some scholars believe that they were the ancestors of the great Maya civilization that followed. Olmec objects and, probably, Olmec influence and religious ideas spread into many areas of the highlands and lowlands, creating the first generalized culture in the region. By 900 B.C. Olmec style and symbols were widely diffused in Mesoamerica." Michael Adas, *The Peoples and Civilizations of the Americas* (1992).

Chapter 19 Exam Options

Option 1 – Matching:

1. Holy Roman Empire: The Central European Empire.
2. Constantinople: New name of the capital of Byzantium.

3. Justinian I: Most famous and capable Byzantium leader.

4. Legal Precedence: Civil law procedure enhanced by Justinian reforms.

5. Civil Law: Law relating to property, not criminal activity.

6. Bubonic Plague: A bacterial infection that devastated Europe.

7. Eastern Orthodox Church: The Eastern Catholic Church with a patriarch at Constantinople.

8. Excommunication: To be cast out of the church and its fellowship.

9. Pandemics: Massive, international outbreaks of disease.

10. Anti-Semites: People who are prejudiced against Jews.

Option 2 – Essay:

Even though the Byzantine intellectual firmly believed that civilization ended with the boundaries of his world, he opened it to all people groups, provided that the latter would join the Eastern Orthodox Church. So, the church was the primary unifying agent in the empire!

Chapter 20 Exam Options

Option 1 – Matching:

1. Slavic Tribes: Ancient middle European tribes who settled in Russia.

2. Germanic Tribes: Central European tribes.

3. Volga Steppes: Rolling hills around the longest river in Europe.

4. Kiev: The capital of a 400-year Kevan Rus Empire.

5. Cossacks: Central Asian fierce warriors who lived on the steppes.

6. Moscow: Capital of Romanov Russia.

7. Romanov Dynasty: The longest Russian ruling family.

8. Ural Mountains: Important mountain range in Russia.

9. Caucasus Mountains: Mountains in southern Russia.

10. Vikings: Scandinavian Norsemen who ravaged Europe and Russia.

Option 2 – Essay:

Western historians generally wrote history until the 20th century and they simply were not going to highlight a Slavic nations, Christian or not!

Chapter 21 Exam Options

Option 1 – Matching:

1. Huns: Powerful barbarian tribe in Eastern Europe.

2. Visigoths: Gothic barbarians.

3. Ostrogoths: Gothic people who mostly lived in Germany.

4. Magyars: Gothic people who lived in Czechoslovakia.

5. Dacians: Ancient Transylvanian people.

6. Bulgars: Ancestors of Bulgaria.

7. Attila: Leader of the Huns.

8. Bishop of Margus: Roman bishop who negotiated with Attila.

9. Ukraine: Central Russian province.

10. Cossacks: Fierce warriors who lived in Eastern Europe and southern Russia.

Option 2 – Essay:

Ethnic nationalism considers the people as a group of physically related persons, a kinship group. "Blood lines" and race are important to ethnic nationalists, who view the nation as an extension of the family or clan. The ideology of Nazi Germany is an extreme example of ethnic nationalism. Ethnic nationalism tended to glorify the past. Ethnic nationalists generates a great deal of xenophobia (fear of outsiders).

Chapter 22 Exam Options

Option 1 – Matching:

1. Passover: Jewish religious celebration.

2. Archetypal: A type.

3. Mastiff: A large breed dog.

4. King Arthur: Mythical Briton King.

5. Robin Hood: Mythical English hero.

6. Prester John: Imaginary historical figure.

7. Pergamon: Or Pergamum was a Greek city in Turkey.

8. Parchment: High quality paper.

9. Papyrus: Paper.

10. Charlemagne: Famous Holy Roman emperor.

Option 2 – Essay:

History is an unfolding of God's plan for the world. Therefore it has purpose. Augustine argued that the rise and fall of empires depended on the designs of Providence.

Chapter 23 Exam Options

Option 1 – Matching:

1. Celts: Germanic tribe that occupied England.
2. Picts: Wild Germanic tribe in Scotland.
3. Britons: Indigenous group mix of Britons and Celts.
4. Anglo-Saxons: German group that invaded and conquered England.
5. Alfred the Great: The greatest Anglo-Saxon king.
6. Domesday Book: First Norman census of England.
7. Magna Carta: Major declaration of the rights of Englishmen.
8. King John: King when Magna Carta was signed.
9. Charter of Liberties: Written and signed by King Henry I after the Magna Carta.
10. Constitutional Law: Law and legislation based on a written document.

Option 2 – Essay:

The Romans were empire builders on a mission to spread their civilization to barbarian lands. One such was Britain, which consisted of various unruly Celtic tribes in conflict with each other (a situation the Romans exploited). Julius Caesar's attempts, in 55 and 54 BC to occupy Britain were defeated by bad weather. Augustus threatened, but never carried out, invasions in 34, 27 and 25 BC. In AD 43, the unpopular Emperor Claudius finally managed. The Romans landed on the south coast and swept through the south, with fierce fighting that drove the British northwest. By AD 50, southern Britain was conquered. London soon became capital of the new province, Britannia. The influence of occupation on British culture was enormous. Roman customs, laws and religions were adopted, while the Romans introduced public baths and exercise areas, central heating and a road system still used today.

Chapter 24 Exam Options

Option 1 – Matching:

1. Bedouin: Nomads who were food gatherers.
2. Koran: The sacred book of Islam.
3. Muhammad: Founder of Islam.
4. Abyssinia: Ethiopia.
5. Wailing Wall: Remaining wall of the destroyed temple.
6. 9/11: Attack on America by Islamic fundamentalists.
7. Islamic Fundamentalism: Militant Islam.
8. Modernity: Movement starting in 1900 that posits that science is most important.
9. A.D. 571: The date of Muhammad's birth.
10. Mecca: City near where Muhammad was born.

Option 2 – Essay:

Both prayers are similar. The Lord's prayer, however, implies a sovereign God who is involved with the affairs of mankind: "thy will be done on earth as it is in heaven." Allah is distant. The Christian prayer invokes a more compassionate deity — one who is compassionate, and understanding. Allah is developed as all-powerful and somewhat distant. Both prayers draw the believer into the presence of the deity, which is an important event. The notion of a "Kingdom come" is alien to the Fatitha. Likewise, "thy will be done" is also alien to the Islamic notion of fate (vs. sovereignty of God).

Chapter 25 Exam Options

Option 1 – Matching:

1. Caliphs: Islamic head of state.
2. Umayyad: Ruling Islamic family.
3. Sunni: The Orthodox Islamic type.
4. Shiites: An Islamic type.
5. Battle of Tours: The battle that stopped Islamic expansion into Europe.
6. Horse Archer: Islamic soldier.
7. Abu al-Qasin: Famous Islamic doctor.
8. Arabesque: A type of calligraphy.
9. Ottoman Empire: Turkish Islamic Empire.
10. Sacrament: Sacred reenactment of the Eucharist, of the last meal that Christ took with his disciples.

Option 2 – Essay:

The Abbasid, ruled most of the Muslim world from 750 to 1258. The city of Baghdad was built in 762 as the capital of the new Caliph, Abu-al-Abbas, a descendant of the Prophet's uncle. The fall of the Umayyad Dynasty marked the end of Arab domination within Islam; the Abbasid caliph made great effort to establish equalitarian treatment of all Islams. This event would be similar to the Diaspora (or spreading around the world) of Judaism. The location of a new capital at Baghdad shifted Islam's center of gravity to the province of Iraq, whose soil, watered by the Tigris and Euphrates, had nurtured the earliest human civilization. The Abbasid Dynasty marked the high point of Islamic power and civilization. The empire ruled by these caliphs was greater in size than the domain of the Roman Caesars; it was the product of an expansion during which the

Muslims assimilated peoples, customs, cultures, and inventions on an unprecedented scale. This Islamic state, in fact, drew from the resources of the entire known world. (Based partly on "Islamic Rule to 1300" by Peter Stearns, George Madison University)

Chapter 26 Exam Options

Option 1 – Matching:

1. Pyrenees Mountains: Mountains separating Spain from the rest of Europe.
2. Strait of Gibraltar: The short body of water separating Africa from Spain.
3. Bay of Biscay: North eastern bay mostly in France.
4. Iberians: Spanish tribes.
5. Basques: Northern Spanish tribes near the Pyrenees.
6. Charles Martel: Frankish king who defeated the Moors at Tours.
7. Philip II: Spanish king who launched the Armada.
8. Armada: Futile Spanish attempt to conquer England in 1599.
9. Moorish Spain: Islamic Spain.
10. Martel: The one who stopped the Moors from conquering Western Europe.

Option 2 – Essay:
Answers will vary.

Chapter 27 Exam Options

Option 1 – Matching:

1. Teutonic Tribes: Germanic tribes.
2. Franks: Barbarian tribes that lived in present-day France.
3. Code of Chivalry: An unwritten code of courtesy.
4. Pages: Six- or seven-year-old apprentices to be knights.
5. Squires: Twelve- to fourteen-year-old apprentices to be knights.
6. Barons: Nobles in a feudal society.
7. Peasants: Poor landless serfs.
8. Serfs: Peasants.
9. Norsemen: Scandinavian peoples.
10. Viking Age: An age when Vikings conquered most of Europe.

Option 2 – Essay:
During the Middle Ages, mounted knights were the chief combatants, though they normally had supporters—men who fought as foot soldiers. The knights were the rulers of the Middle Ages, and from their position of wealth and power emerged the social system called feudalism. As long as they could fight and win battles, and offer society protection, they were positioned in places of influence. Nearly all the great armies of the period were dominated by cavalry groups of knights. That would end with gunpowder. The resurgence of the foot soldier came with the introduction of gunpowder. The minie ball ended the effectiveness of cavalry as a weapon forever.

Chapter 28 Exam Options

Option 1 – Matching:

1. Cottage Industries: Industries that occurred in individual homes.
2. Wimple: A woman's head covering.
3. Boroughs: District of a city.
4. Epic: A long narrative about a hero.
5. Song of Roland: An epic narrative about a French hero.
6. Poema del Cid: An epic narrative about a Spanish hero.
7. Divine Comedy: Written by Dante, the first serious literature written in Italian.
8. Canterbury Tales: A fictional piece written by English poet Geoffrey Chaucer.
9. Bourgeois: Inhabitants of the bourgs or burghs.
10. Monogamy: Being faithful to one spouse.

Option 2 – Essay:

The medieval world was not merely a sterile scientific world. It included pictures and decorations. The world to medieval man was much smaller than it really was. Certainly Columbus' explorations, if they proved anything, was that the world was larger than many once thought.

Chapter 29 Exam Options

Option 1 – Matching:

1. Pottage: Thick soup.
2. Humors: Parts of the body temperament.
3. Courtly Love: Medieval code for ladies.
4. Kinship and Patronage: What shaped society in the Middle Ages.
5. Astrology: Constellations and planets were thought to influence.

Option 2 – Essay:

Population increase is inevitably tied to food production. The clearing of land and new techniques in agriculture led to higher food production. Agricultural tools, such as the heavy plow, along with new methods for harnessing animal power, such as the horse collar, enabled farmers to work the rich, dense soil of northern Europe using less labor. The three-field system replaced two-field crop rotation, allowing farmers to cultivate two-thirds, instead of half, of their land at once, while leaving one-third to rest. In the 12th century, energy-producing devices such as the windmill for grinding grain also increased productivity. An improved diet with iron-rich legumes increased women's life span and helped them survive childbearing.

Chapter 30 Exam Options

Option 1 – Matching:

1. Carolingians: First Frankish monarch line.
2. Frankish Kingdom: First medieval European empire.
3. Charlemagne: Charles the Great, ruler of the Holy Roman Empire.
4. Einhard: Friend of Charlemagne, who kept a diary which describes Charlemagne.
5. Pope Leo III: Friend and partner with Charlemagne.
6. Holy Roman Empire: Central European Empire.
7. Eusebius: Early church historian.
8. Homeschooling: The only option of education for the poor at this time.
9. Primary Sources: Firsthand references to words and ideas.
10. Church of St. Peter: A place cherished by Charlemagne.

Option 2 – Essay:

Answers will vary.

Chapter 31 Exam Options

Option 1 – Matching:

1. Gregory the Great: First medieval pope.
2. Parousia: The Second Coming of Christ.
3. Benedictine Monk: The contemplative who founded a monastery order.
4. Bishops: Lower rank of Roman Catholic hierarchy.
5. Archbishops: Higher rank of Roman Catholic hierarchy.

6. Visigoths: Barbarian tribe.
7. Boniface: Apostle to the Germans.
8. Theodoric: King of Ostrogoth people.
9. Cassiodorus: Christian scholar.
10. Scriptoria: Room in a monastery devoted to copying Scripture.

Option 2 – Essay:

The Parson has no physical description other than of his staff, which is a symbol of his role as shepherd over his congregation. Chaucer describes the Parson as "Benign... and wondrous diligent. Patient in adverse times and well content" (7, 8). Chaucer intended the Parson's description to focus on his spiritual depth rather than his physical appearance. The physical description of these characters reflects the lechery of the Friar and the godliness of the Parson. The Parson follows the ethical code that he prescribes to others, namely, God's Word. He also unselfishly cares for his congregation with purity and respect toward each member. The Parson is poor, "but rather would he give... unto those poor... part of his income." The Parson's selfless attitude is seen through his care for his congregation and his desire to live honestly. He was poor in monetary terms, "But rich he was in holy thought and work." Jason Johnson, Chaucer's "Canterbury Tales: Contrasting Clergy."

Chapter 32 Exam Options

Option 1 – Matching:

1. Franciscans: A Roman Catholic monastic order.
2. Cistercian Monastery: A complex for a Roman Catholic monastic order.
3. *Sixteen Revelations of Divine Love*: Written by Julian of Norwich.
4. Mechtild: Wrote poetry and spiritual texts in German.
5. Julian of Norwich: Wrote the book *Sixteen Revelations of Divine Love*.

Option 2 – Essay:

Answers will vary.

Chapter 33 Exam Options

Option 1 – Matching:

1. Saracens: Those whom the crusaders warred against.
2. Italian City States: Bold, sassy, and innovative entities.

3. The Holy Grail: Thought to be the dish, plate, or cup used by Jesus at the Last Supper.
4. Motifs: Themes or ideas.
5. The Teutonic Order: A special group of knights from Germany.

Option 2 – Essay:

Answers will vary; however, in light of September 11, 2011, one has to pause and think.

Chapter 34 Exam Options

Option 1 – Matching:

1. Ferdinand of Aragon: King of Spain after the Moors were driven out.
2. Isabella of Castile: Queen of Spain after the Moors were driven out.
3. October 12, 1492: The day Columbus discovered America.
4. Bartolome de las Casas: Kept a log of Columbus' voyages.
5. Columbus quincentenary of 1992: 500-year anniversary of Columbus' voyage.

Option 2 – Essay:

Clearly this is true. Besides Columbus' voyage there were two other very important events in Spain that same year, involving the Jewish and Muslim (Moor) population of Spain. Conquest of Granada (January 2), the last Muslim stronghold in Spain; completing the reconquest of Spain from Islam/Moor rule; Edict of Expulsion (issued by Ferdinand and Isabella from Granada, March 31) — gave the Jews four months to convert to Christianity or leave Spain.

Parent Lesson Plan — Promotion

Now turn your favorite **Master Books** into curriculum! Each Parent Lesson Plan (PLP) includes:

- ☉ An easy-to-follow, one-year educational calendar
- ☉ Helpful worksheets, quizzes, tests, and answer keys
- ☉ Additional teaching helps and insights
- ☉ Complete with all you need to quickly and easily begin your education program today!

ELEMENTARY ZOOLOGY

1 year
4th – 6th

Package Includes: *World of Animals, Dinosaur Activity Book, The Complete Aquarium Adventure, The Complete Zoo Adventure, Parent Lesson Plan*

5 Book Package
978-0-89051-747-5 $84.99

SCIENCE STARTERS: ELEMENTARY PHYSICAL & EARTH SCIENCE

1 year
3rd – 8th grade

6 Book Package Includes: *Forces & Motion –Student, Student Journal, and Teacher; The Earth – Student, Teacher & Student Journal; Parent Lesson Plan*

6 Book Package
978-0-89051-748-2 $51.99

SCIENCE STARTERS: ELEMENTARY CHEMISTRY & PHYSICS

1 year
3rd – 8th grade

Package Includes: *Matter – Student, Student Journal, and Teacher; Energy – Student, Teacher, & Student Journal; Parent Lesson Plan*

7 Book Package
978-0-89051-749-9 $54.99

INTRO TO METEOROLOGY & ASTRONOMY

1 year
7th – 9th grade
½ Credit

Package Includes: *The Weather Book; The Astronomy Book; Parent Lesson Plan*

3 Book Package
978-0-89051-753-6 $44.99

INTRO TO OCEANOGRAPHY & ECOLOGY

1 year
7th – 9th grade
½ Credit

Package Includes: *The Ocean Book; The Ecology Book; Parent Lesson Plan*

3 Book Package
978-0-89051-754-3 $45.99

INTRO TO SPELEOLOGY & PALEONTOLOGY

1 year
7th – 9th grade
½ Credit

Package Includes: *The Cave Book; The Fossil Book; Parent Lesson Plan*

3 Book Package
978-0-89051-752-9 $44.99

CONCEPTS OF MEDICINE & BIOLOGY

1 year
7th – 9th grade
½ Credit

Package Includes: *Exploring the History of Medicine; Exploring the World of Biology; Parent Lesson Plan*

3 Book Package
978-0-89051-756-7 $40.99

CONCEPTS OF MATHEMATICS & PHYSICS

1 year
7th – 9th grade
½ Credit

Package Includes: *Exploring the World of Mathematics; Exploring the World of Physics; Parent Lesson Plan*

3 Book Package
978-0-89051-757-4 $40.99

CONCEPTS OF EARTH SCIENCE & CHEMISTRY

1 year
7th – 9th grade
½ Credit

Package Includes: *Exploring Planet Earth; Exploring the World of Chemistry; Parent Lesson Plan*

3 Book Package
978-0-89051-755-0 $40.99

THE SCIENCE OF LIFE: BIOLOGY

1 year
8th – 9th grade
½ Credit

Package Includes: *Building Blocks in Science; Building Blocks in Life Science; Parent Lesson Plan*

3 Book Package
978-0-89051-758-1 $44.99

BASIC PRE-MED

1 year
8th – 9th grade
½ Credit

Package Includes: *The Genesis of Germs; The Building Blocks in Life Science; Parent Lesson Plan*

3 Book Package
978-0-89051-759-8 $43.99

INTRO TO ASTRONOMY

1 year
7th – 9th grade
½ Credit

Package Includes: *The Stargazer's Guide to the Night Sky; Parent Lesson Plan*

2 Book Package
978-0-89051-760-4 $47.99

INTRO TO ARCHAEOLOGY & GEOLOGY

1 year
7th – 9th
½ Credit

Package Includes: *The Archaeology Book; The Geology Book; Parent Lesson Plan*

3 Book Package
978-0-89051-751-2 $45.99

SURVEY OF SCIENCE HISTORY & CONCEPTS

1 year
10th – 12th grade
1 Credit

Package Includes: *The World of Mathematics; The World of Physics; The World of Biology; The World of Chemistry; Parent Lesson Plan*

5 Book Package
978-0-89051-764-2 $72.99

SURVEY OF SCIENCE SPECIALTIES

1 year
10th – 12th grade
1 Credit

Package Includes: *The Cave Book; The Fossil Book; The Geology Book; The Archaeology Book; Parent Lesson Plan*

5 Book Package
978-0-89051-765-9 $81.99

SURVEY OF ASTRONOMY

1 year
10th – 12th grade
1 Credit

Package Includes: *The Stargazers Guide to the Night Sky; Our Created Moon; Taking Back Astronomy; Our Created Moon DVD; Created Cosmos DVD; Parent Lesson Plan*

4 Book, 2 DVD Package
978-0-89051-766-6 $113.99

GEOLOGY & BIBLICAL HISTORY

1 year
8th – 9th
1 Credit

Package Includes: *Explore the Grand Canyon; Explore Yellowstone; Explore Yosemite & Zion National Parks; Your Guide to the Grand Canyon; Your Guide to Yellowstone; Your Guide to Zion & Bryce Canyon National Parks; Parent Lesson Plan.*

4 Book, 3 DVD Package
978-0-89051-750-5 $108.99

PALEONTOLOGY: LIVING FOSSILS

1 year
10th – 12th grade
½ Credit

Package Includes: *Living Fossils, Living Fossils Teacher Guide, Living Fossils DVD; Parent Lesson Plan*

3 Book, 1 DVD Package
978-0-89051-763-5 $66.99

LIFE SCIENCE ORIGINS & SCIENTIFIC THEORY

1 year
10th – 12th grade
1 Credit

Package Includes: *Evolution: the Grand Experiment, Teacher Guide, DVD; Living Fossils, Teacher Guide, DVD; Parent Lesson Plan*

5 Book, 2 DVD Package
978-0-89051-761-1 $144.99

NATURAL SCIENCE THE STORY OF ORIGINS

1 year
10th – 12th grade
½ Credit

Package Includes: *Evolution: the Grand Experiment; Evolution: the Grand Experiment Teacher's Guide, Evolution: the Grand Experiment DVD; Parent Lesson Plan*

3 Book, 1 DVD Package
978-0-89051-762-8 $71.99

ADVANCED PRE-MED STUDIES

1 year
10th – 12th grade
1 Credit

Package Includes: *Building Blocks in Life Science; The Genesis of Germs; Body by Design; Exploring the History of Medicine; Parent Lesson Plan*

5 Book Package
978-0-89051-767-3 $76.99

BIBLICAL ARCHAEOLOGY

1 year
10th – 12th grade
1 Credit

Package Includes: *Unwrapping the Pharaohs; Unveiling the Kings of Israel; The Archaeology Book; Parent Lesson Plan.*

4 Book Package
978-0-89051-768-0 $99.99

CHRISTIAN HERITAGE

1 year
10th – 12th grade
1 Credit

Package Includes: *For You They Signed; Lesson Parent Plan*

2 Book Package
978-0-89051-769-7 $50.99